D0893338

▶ **Taking Evil Seriously**

DOI: 10.1057/9781137412669.0001

Other Palgrave Pivot titles

Ian I. Mitroff: The Crisis-Prone Society: A Brief Guide to Managing the Beliefs That Drive Risk in Business

Takis S. Pappas: Populism and Crisis Politics in Greece

G. Douglas Atkins: T.S. Eliot and the Fulfillment of Christian Poetics

Guri Tyldum and Lisa G. Johnston (editor): Applying Respondent Driven Sampling to Migrant Populations: Lessons from the Field

Shoon Murray: The Terror Authorization: The History and Politics of the 2001 AUMF

Irene Zempi and Neil Chakraborti: Islamophobia, Victimisation and the Veil

Duggan, Marian and Vicky Heap: Administrating Victimization: The Politics of Anti-Social Behaviour and Hate Crime Policy

Pamela J. Stewart and Andrew J. Strathern: Working in the Field: Anthropological Experiences across the World

Audrey Foster Gwendolyn: Hoarders, Doomsday Preppers, and the Culture of Apocalypse

Sue Ellen Henry: Children's Bodies in Schools: Corporeal Performances of Social Class

Max J. Skidmore: Maligned Presidents: The Late 19th Century

Lynée Lewis Gaillet and Letizia Guglielmo: Scholarly Publication in a Changing Academic Landscape

Owen Anderson: Reason and Faith at Early Princeton: Piety and the Knowledge of God

Mark L. Robinson: Marketing Big Oil: Brand Lessons from the World's Largest Companies

Nicholas Robinette: Realism, Form and the Postcolonial Novel

Andreosso-O'Callaghan, Bernadette, Jacques Jaussaud, and Maria Bruna Zolin (editors): Economic Integration in Asia: Towards the Delineation of a Sustainable Path

Umut Özkırımlı: The Making of a Protest Movement in Turkey: #occupygezi

Ilan Bijaoui: The Economic Reconciliation Process: Middle Eastern Populations in Conflict

Leandro Rodriguez Medina: The Circulation of European Knowledge: Niklas Luhmann in the Hispanic Americas

Terje Rasmussen: Personal Media and Everyday Life: A Networked Lifeworld

Nikolay Anguelov: Policy and Political Theory in Trade Practices: Multinational Corporations and Global Governments

Sirpa Salenius: Rose Elizabeth Cleveland: First Lady and Literary Scholar

Sten Vikner and Eva Engels: Scandinavian Object Shift and Optimality Theory

Chris Rumford: Cosmopolitan Borders

Majid Yar: The Cultural Imaginary of the Internet: Virtual Utopias and Dystopias

Vanita Sundaram: Preventing Youth Violence: Rethinking the Role of Gender and Schools

Giampaolo Viglia: Pricing, Online Marketing Behavior, and Analytics

Nicos Christodoulakis: Germany's War Debt to Greece: A Burden Unsettled

Volker H. Schmidt: Global Modernity. A Conceptual Sketch

Mayesha Alam: Women and Transitional Justice: Progress and Persistent Challenges in Retributive and Restorative Processes

DOI: 10.1057/9781137412669.0001

palgrave▶pivot

Taking Evil Seriously

▶

Sami Pihlström

Professor of Philosophy of Religion,
University of Helsinki, Finland

palgrave
macmillan

DOI: 10.1057/9781137412669

First published by 2014
PALGRAVE MACMILLAN

Palgrave Macmillan in the UK is an imprint of Macmillan Publishers Limited, registered in England, company number 785998, of Houndmills, Basingstoke, Hampshire RG21 6XS.

Palgrave Macmillan in the US is a division of St Martin's Press LLC, 175 Fifth Avenue, New York, NY 10010.

Palgrave Macmillan is the global academic imprint of the above companies and has companies and representatives throughout the world.

Palgrave® and Macmillan® are registered trademarks in the United States, the United Kingdom, Europe and other countries

ISBN: 978-1-137-41267-6 EPUB
ISBN: 978-1-137-41266-9 PDF
ISBN: 978-1-137-41265-2 Hardback

This book is printed on paper suitable for recycling and made from fully managed and sustained forest sources. Logging, pulping and manufacturing processes are expected to conform to the environmental regulations of the country of origin.

A catalogue record for this book is available from the British Library.

A catalog record for this book is available from the Library of Congress.

www.palgrave.com/pivot

DOI: 10.1057/9781137412669

▶ Incompatibility of the future with their desires and active tendencies is, in fact, to most men a source of more fixed disquietude than uncertainty itself. Witness the attempts to overcome the 'problem of evil', the 'mystery of pain'. There is no 'problem of good'.

William James,
'The Sentiment of Rationality' (1879),
The Will to Believe and Other Essays in Popular Philosophy
(Cambridge, MA and London: Harvard University Press,
1979), p. 70

DOI: 10.1057/9781137412669.0001

Contents

DOI: 10.1057/9781137412669.0001

Acknowledgments

Fragments of this material have been presented at conferences and other events, home and abroad. Paper presentations and lectures at the following institutions in 2012–2014 have been particularly important for the development of my ideas: Helsinki Collegium for Advanced Studies (University of Helsinki, Finland); the Philosophical Society of Finland; Max-Weber-Kolleg (University of Erfurt, Germany); Polish University of Humanities and Social Sciences (Wroclaw, Poland); Faculty of Theology, Uppsala University (Sweden); 23rd World Congress of Philosophy (Athens, Greece); Templeton Summer School on theological realism (Mainz, Germany); and Peter Wall Institute for Advanced Studies (University of British Columbia, Vancouver, Canada).

An article upon which some parts of Chapter 2 are based will appear in Hermann Deuser, Hans Joas, Matthias Jung, and Magnus Schlette (eds), *The Challenge of Contingency and the Significance of Transcendence: Classical Pragmatism and the Theory of Religion* (a volume based on a conference organized at the Max-Weber-Kolleg, Erfurt, in 2012), to be published by Fordham University Press. Some fragments of the chapter are also partly based on an essay forthcoming in Leszek Koczanowicz and Wojciech Malecki (eds), *Rethinking Pragmatist Aesthetics* (a volume based on a conference organized in Wroclaw in 2012). An early version of Chapter 3 appeared, with the title, 'Jonas and James: The Ethics and Metaphysics of Post-Holocaust Pragmatism', in *The Journal of Speculative Philosophy*, vol. 28, no. 1 (2014) (© Pennsylvania State University Press). I am most grateful to the editors and publishers of these books and journals for the permission to use copyrighted material. None of these previous conference or journal papers is reprinted here as such. Even in those cases in which earlier material has been used, the chapters have been significantly revised and rewritten.

The friends and colleagues whose critical comments I have benefited from are too numerous to be thanked individually. Let me just mention some of those philosophers and other scholars whose influence has, I think, left identifiable traces in this volume: Richard Bernstein, Vincent Colapietro, the late Michael Eldridge, Dirk-Martin Grube, Sara Heinämaa, Ana Honnacker, Hans Joas, Heikki Kannisto, Sari Kivistö, Heikki J. Koskinen, Heikki A. Kovalainen, Joseph Margolis, Olli-Pekka Moisio, Wayne Proudfoot, Joel Robbins, Henrik Rydenfelt, Risto Saarinen, Thomas Schmidt, the late Juha Sihvola, Emil Višňovský, and Ulf Zackariasson. More specific intellectual debts will be acknowledged in their particular contexts.

This book was written during the past couple of years of my term as the Director of the Helsinki Collegium for Advanced Studies. I am grateful to this wonderful institution which I have had the privilege of developing for five years, and particularly to Maija Väätämöinen, one of our excellent research assistants, who helped me in the final stages of putting the manuscript together. Finally, I would like to acknowledge the continuous support of my family, even though I am also sad about the fact that my children, like all of us, have to grow up in a world in which evil does have to be taken seriously.

Sami Pihlström
Helsinki, February 2014

Introduction

Pihlström, Sami. *Taking Evil Seriously*. Basingstoke: Palgrave Macmillan, 2014. DOI: 10.1057/9781137412669.0003.

▶

The American philosopher and psychologist William James (1842–1910) coined the puzzling notion of a 'moral holiday.' He famously argued in *Pragmatism: A New Name for Some Old Ways of Thinking* (1907) that the only pragmatic function that Hegelian philosophers' favorite metaphysical postulate, the 'Absolute,' could serve is that it might occasionally grant us a moral holiday, an opportunity to think that everything is, in the end, well and fine without our attempts to contribute to the moral progress or ultimate salvation of the world. James, however, firmly rejected such an easy solution to the problem of evil and suffering. On the contrary, a truly ethical attitude, he reminded us, requires full recognition of the reality of evil and suffering.

Taking evil seriously entails that our moral holidays are inevitably plagued by a certain kind of insomnia, an inability to rest. Instead of James's views, the notion of insomnia here refers to a quite different philosophical framework, that is, the French philosopher Emmanuel Levinas's ethics, which requires the ethical subject to be constantly 'awake,' ready to take up the infinite challenge of facing the irreducible otherness of the other person.

I was initially planning to title this work *Insomnia on a Moral Holiday*. Even though I in the end chose an easier title directly introducing the topic, the original title also leads us to the main themes of the work. The present book is largely concerned with the way in which moral philosophy, or *any morally serious philosophy*, should react to the undeniable presence of evil and suffering. In brief, I will argue that moral philosophy, or morally serious philosophy, should begin from the recognition of the reality of evil. It thus has a 'negative' task and is inevitably engaged in what we may more generally call 'negative thinking.' This point needs to be emphasized, because moral philosophy has since antiquity been primarily understood as a 'positive' examination of the good life.

Thus, I have two main aims in this short book. First, I will articulate and defend the basic ideas of what I call 'negative thinking' in general, hoping to show why we should focus on negative concepts instead of positive ones, especially in moral philosophy – or, arguably, any morally serious philosophy. The most central, and most serious, negative concept I will try to deal with in these chapters is the notion of *evil*. I will apply a Peircean account of 'real generals' to the problem of evil: according to this proposal, evil is a 'general' instead of being something particular, although of course it mostly manifests itself in particular cases and often in its shocking concreteness. This view, as will be explained in

DOI: 10.1057/9781137412669.0003

Chapter 1, is derived from Charles S. Peirce's 'extreme scholastic realism,' which postulates real generals such as habits and dispositions, without reducing them to existing particulars. I will also argue that 'theodicist' attempts to justify the reality of evil – that is, philosophies that seek a theodicy, either religious or secular – are ethically disastrous.

Secondly, my goal is to develop a broadly Jamesian pragmatist approach to the reality of evil and suffering as a fundamental challenge to moral thought. In the interest of articulating and defending such an approach, I will also compare William James's views to thinkers not typically associated with Jamesian pragmatism: Ludwig Wittgenstein and Paul Feyerabend (Chapter 2), as well as Hans Jonas (Chapter 3). These comparisons will shed further light on James's pragmatism – in James's own pluralistic and open spirit.

My thesis about the priority of the concept of evil to the concept of the good should not be misunderstood. Let me therefore note that I am fully happy with, say, *anthropology* focusing on the good – yielding a perhaps inevitable cultural relativism, or at least pluralism, given the differing conceptions of the good in different cultures and societies – while insisting on the idea that *moral philosophy*, or (again) more generally any morally serious philosophy (whether it is strictly speaking 'moral philosophy' or not), ought to focus on evil, with no relief available from any relativism about the good. One problem here is how we can be relativists about a culture-embedded concept (the good) while rejecting relativism about its conceptual contrast (evil). My proposed solution will be a pragmatist – Peircean-Jamesian – account of evil, which I will develop by starting from the classical pragmatists' writings but by going considerably beyond their own views.

I also have aims internal to pragmatism scholarship. Most importantly, my reflections can be seen as an attempt to reflect on the so-called *pragmatic method* itself. It can be argued that Peirce's original Pragmatic Maxim, which urges us to consider what conceivable practical bearings the objects of our conception may have and then to conclude that our conception of those bearings is 'the whole of our conception of the object,' is either too restrictive or else void or trivial.[1] On the one hand, if we really strictly require the objects of our theories and conceptions to have practical bearings, then certain skeptical scenarios, for instance, won't make sense at all – it is precisely their point that they should *not* make any practical difference to our daily activities. Even though we may be convinced that philosophical skepticism is pointless, we should

DOI: 10.1057/9781137412669.0003

hardly simply regard, say, 'Brains in a Vat' type of problems as *meaningless*.[2] Here the pragmatic method appears to be *too restrictive*. On the other hand, if the pragmatic principle is liberalized, in William James's manner, to cover not only the conceivable bearings of the objects of our conception but also the bearings of our beliefs, ideas, or concepts themselves, then this specific problem will not arise: it may, clearly, make a dramatic difference for us in our lives whether we believe in a skeptical scenario (even hypothetically) or not. Our attitudes, emotions, and beliefs obviously make a huge difference to our lives. But then the pragmatic method may turn out to be *too loose*: can we just believe whatever we find most rewarding or subjectively satisfying in life; are there any even relatively objective normative criteria for the legitimacy of such beliefs?

This book cannot settle any major problems in pragmatism scholarship. I have explored pragmatism – including the classical pragmatists Peirce and James, as well as their pragmatic method and its different versions – on a number of earlier occasions.[3] What I hope to do here is to *sharpen* the pragmatic method by relating it to the 'negativity' idea I will defend in Chapter 1. This, at least, is proposed as *one* possible way of making the pragmatic method more precise and efficient in the kind of ethico-religious, or *'weltanschaulichen,'* concerns that James himself was troubled by. The key point is that the way our ideas and/or their objects make a difference in our lives, and in human culture more generally, is, at least mostly or most importantly, through their negative effects. We therefore must, in order to truly examine the ways in which our thought and ideas make a moral difference to the world, focus on evil instead of the good effects those ideas may have; very simply, the 'difference-making' power of evil is much more dramatic, and it is only against the background provided by evil that goodness can shine. So what I am offering is a reflection on the kind of difference-making we should be philosophically concerned with – whether or not we subscribe to the pragmatic method generally or not. As I will explain, this will also enable us to (re)connect the pragmatic method with the *transcendental method*: we are ultimately concerned with certain necessary conditions for the possibility of moral agency and the moral point of view itself, with what we need to presuppose to make sense of ourselves as moral agents.[4]

The book will, accordingly, transcendentally examine how the pragmatic method, seeking to articulate the true meaning of our concepts,

DOI: 10.1057/9781137412669.0003

conceptions, ideas, and theories in terms of the conceivable practical effects of their objects, should focus on negative (rather than positive) ethical concepts, such as evil, as the effects of *their* objects are much more directly, and often shockingly, available in our individual and communal experience. The reason why this investigation can and should be called 'transcendental' is that it is precisely this sharpening of the pragmatic method that opens up the entire horizon of what is morally possible for us as human beings. My pragmatic-transcendental method has also *metaphysical* relevance: it is ultimately about the way the human world is constituted through ethical engagement. Metaphysics, as pragmatists like James have urged, is in the end based on ethics.[5] I will reinforce this Jamesian point by examining the link between the metaphysical and ethical dimensions of ethical negativity. I propose to do this through broadly Jamesian pragmatism, though I must hasten to add that even those parts of the book that are most directly concerned with James do not aim at a detailed scholarly interpretation of what I take James to have 'really said.' I will argue, drawing from James, that a negative approach in moral philosophy leads to an understanding of human beings' place in the world that might be described as *melancholic*, or an understanding that acknowledges the 'tragic sense of life' – to quote a Spanish thinker whom James influenced, Miguel de Unamuno. Ethics, in this sense, is not primarily, or perhaps not at all, a matter of rules or principles but a matter of a proper attitude, bad conscience, and guilt. In this sense, Jamesian pragmatism can be shown to focus on and further develop philosophical ideas that might have been thought to be available only in the so-called Continental tradition in contemporary philosophy.

The following pages will, moreover, address not merely an *intellectual* difficulty or challenge but also an *existential* difficulty and, of course, an *ethical* one. We are not only dealing with philosophical arguments and concepts but also with an experience we may have when encountering evil, suffering, death, and other 'negativities' of human life: that is, the experience that somehow our concepts are, and always will be, inadequate to the kind of world we live in and the kind of experiences we need to deal with. This problem of what might be called the *existential (in)adequacy of conceptualization* leads us to consider evil and other negativities from a perhaps slightly unusual perspective. It is to such consideration that we will turn in the following chapters, keeping ethico-existential and metaphysico-theological perspectives closely integrated.

DOI: 10.1057/9781137412669.0003

Before moving on to a more detailed discussion of evil and negativity from the point of view of the pragmatic method, it is necessary to add a general characterization of the pragmatic method itself, understood as a method of (philosophical but not only philosophical) *inquiry*. How does, or how should, the pragmatist thinker understand the concept of inquiry (in general terms)? We may begin from the pragmatists' resolute *anti-Cartesianism*. While René Descartes, famously, started by doubting everything that can be doubted and arrived at the 'Archimedean point' at which, allegedly, doubt is no longer possible – the doubting and thinking subject's self-discovery, *cogito, ergo sum* – Peirce's anti-Cartesian essays in the 1860–70s dramatically questioned the very possibility of this traditional approach to epistemology.[6] Skipping the details of Peirce's arguments here, we may say that we can never begin from complete doubt; on the contrary, we always have to start our inquiries from the beliefs we already possess. There is no way of *living* – no way of 'being-in-the-world,' to use terminology well known in a very different philosophical tradition, that is, Heideggerian phenomenology – in the absence of *believing*, that is, holding certain beliefs to be true about the world, at least one's more or less immediate surroundings with which one is in constant interaction. Doubt does play a role in inquiry, but it is subordinate to belief. Therefore, global skepticism is pragmatically a non-starter, even if it is not, strictly speaking, meaningless.

Moreover, beliefs themselves are *habits of action* – and this of course is a key pragmatist point, also shared by those pragmatists that may not be as helpful as Peirce in developing a theory of inquiry, including especially James.[7] Beliefs do not just give rise to habits of action, but they quite literally *are* such habits. To believe something to be the case is always already to act in the world in a way or another, and not only to concretely act but also to be *prepared* to act in certain ways should certain types of situations arise. Pragmatism, thus, does not reduce our beliefs to actions but more generally proposes to rearticulate the very notion of believing as a notion ineliminably tied up with the notion of habitual action.[8]

In the emergence of inquiry, the crucial step is taken when something goes wrong, that is, when a habit does *not* function smoothly, when our action is interrupted or yields a surprise – a certain kind of 'negativity' thus again playing a key role here. Then, and only then, does doubt enter the process. The surprise leads to genuine doubt (instead of the

Cartesian 'paper doubt' that Peirce ridiculed), a state of doubt that is directed to the original belief(s) that gave rise to, or better *were*, the habit(s) of action that led to the surprise. The purpose of the inquiry that then naturally follows is to settle that doubt and to fix a new belief or set of beliefs that do not yield the same kind of surprising result that the original belief(s) and/or habit(s) of action did. Through this process of inquiry, the original belief(s) and/or habit(s) are either revised or replaced by new and better ones. The way John Dewey describes inquiry as an intelligent response to problematic situations that need to be transformed into unproblematic ones is essentially similar, though by and large somewhat more naturalistically phrased, emphasizing inquiry as a continuous 'transaction' between a living organism and its environment.[9]

How, then, does an inquiry, pragmatically conceived, proceed in seeking to terminate doubt and fix (new) belief? Peirce's examination of the 'fixation of belief' is the pragmatist *locus classicus* here, even though the term 'pragmatism' does not yet appear in the 1877 essay, 'The Fixation of Belief.' Famously, Peirce rejects the three methods of fixing belief he finds unsatisfactory for various reasons – that is, what he calls the methods of tenacity and authority, as well as the 'intuitive' method of what is 'agreeable to reason' – and defends the *scientific method* as the only method capable of truly rational belief-fixation in the long run. The distinctive feature of the scientific method in comparison to the inferior methods is that it lets the 'real things' that are independent of us – that is, independent of the inquirers and their beliefs or opinions[10] – influence the way in which our new beliefs are fixed. Our beliefs must thus be responsive to our experiences of the world that is largely independent of us in order for them to be properly scientific. A key idea to be developed in the present work is that we must be responsive to the reality of evil, in particular, in order to be able to engage in moral inquiry at all.

Peirce's theory of the progress of scientific inquiry is also well known: if the ideal community of rational inquirers (who need not be human) were able to engage in inquiry, using the scientific method, for an indefinitely long time, its beliefs regarding any given question would converge to an ideal 'final opinion.' This final opinion will, however, never be actually achieved; it is an ideal end, a matter of 'would' rather than of 'will.' The same holds for the kind of moral reflection and inquiry whose possibility I am examining here: the task of responding to evil is endless,

DOI: 10.1057/9781137412669.0003

never to be actually completed, opening us again and again to a future that sets us infinite tasks.

Now, how does the Peircean-Deweyan pragmatist conception of science and inquiry accommodate *non-scientific* inquiries, such as the 'existential' philosophical inquiry we are about to begin in this book? One way of approaching this question is by asking whether the pragmatist conception of inquiry is *monistic* or *pluralistic*. Does it, that is, seek to provide us with the *essence* of inquiry?

These questions are difficult to answer unless we make the relevant terms clear. It is, I think, helpful to view inquiry as a 'family-resemblance' notion in Ludwig Wittgenstein's sense without any permanent and fixed essence.[11] There are, as we know, quite different inquiries in different areas of life, from our everyday affairs to science as well as art, politics, ethics, and religion, and many other practices. There is no pragmatic need, or point, to force all these quite different modes of inquiry into the same model. In this sense, pragmatism definitely defends a pluralistic conception of inquiry. However, it can simultaneously be maintained that very different inquiries share a similar pragmatic method, that is, the 'doubt-belief' method sketched above (as it has often been called) and the related scientific method (as distinguished from the inferior methods Peirce attacks). The movement from habits of actions and beliefs through surprise and doubt to inquiry and to new or revised beliefs and habits is general enough to allow an indefinite amount of contextual variation. A certain kind of *context-sensitivity* is, then, a crucial feature of pragmatism – not only of pragmatist theories of inquiry but of pragmatism more generally. Even if we can say that the 'same' pragmatist account of inquiry can be applied to inquiries taking place in very different contexts, or different human practices (including practices we would prefer to call non-scientific), this is only the beginning of our inquiry into inquiry. The notion of inquiry will be pragmatically clarified – its pragmatic meaning will be properly brought into view – only when its local contexts are made clear.

Moreover, when those contexts *are* made clear, it no longer matters very much whether we call the methods used 'scientific' or not. This is mostly a terminological matter (though it is also important to keep in mind that terminological issues are often not at all trivial). We may, that is, employ Peirce's 'scientific method' also when we are not pursuing science literally speaking. Political discussion, for instance, may be 'scientific' in the relevant pragmatist sense if it is genuinely open to belief-revision in the face of recalcitrant experience, argument, and evidence, even if it does not aim at scientific-like results. If it is not open-minded in this way, or if it is, rather, based on stubborn ideological opinions never to be changed no matter what happens, it is simply not a form of inquiry at all. Obviously, this also holds for the present undertaking.

I would like to suggest that we leave the concept of inquiry, quite deliberately, vague enough to cover inquiries that do not 'pursue truth' in the sense in which scientific and more generally academic and/or scholarly inquiries can be regarded as pursuing the truth. We should of course admit that the pursuit of truth is a pervasive phenomenon in academic life, not only in the natural sciences but also in those areas of inquiry (say, literary criticism) where truth itself is largely a matter of interpretation or, for instance, construction of new illuminating perspectives on certain historical documents.[12] But we should also admit that inquiry extends even to areas in which it no longer makes much sense to speak about the pursuit of truth.[13] For instance, political discussion may take the form of an inquiry as long as the participants are responsive to each others' possibly conflicting ideas and the evidence and other considerations brought to the picture by the discussants. Artistic inquiries, in turn, may very interestingly question our received views and conceptualizations of the world (including the place of academic inquiry in our world), often much more effectively than scientific theory-formation ever can. And even religious 'inquiries' into one's most fundamental ways of relating to the world and to one's individual and communal lives may deserve the honorific title of an inquiry even if they are never responsive to evidence in the way science is but are, rather, primarily just responsive to the existential needs of the subject and the satisfaction of those needs in that person's concrete life situations.[14]

While this book does not primarily deal with religion, this existential tone is also central to the kind of ethico-metaphysical inquiry, in a pragmatist spirit equipped with transcendental dimensions, that I am about to begin. I do hope my use of the pragmatic method will constitute a self-reflective inquiry critically explicating and transforming that method itself. Whether I will be able to arrive at any truths, or even candidates for truth, will be for other inquirers to judge. By briefly characterizing the pragmatist conception of inquiry in this introduction I have merely wanted to emphasize that there is no a priori reason to exclude a moral reflection such as the one to be offered in the following chapters from the family of human practices we call 'inquiries.'

DOI: 10.1057/9781137412669.0003

Notes

1 I was brought to see the relevance of this general problem regarding the pragmatic method to my particular concerns in this inquiry after an interesting conversation with Professor Marcus Willaschek. See also later sections of this introduction for a somewhat more detailed account of the pragmatic method. For Willaschek's own examination of pragmatism as a way of transforming metaphysics – especially toward a reflection on human contingency – see Marcus Willaschek, 'Bedingtes Vertrauen: Auf dem Weg zu einer pragmatistischen Transformation der Metaphysik' in Martin Hartmann, Jasper Liptow, and Marcus Willaschek (eds), *Die Gegenwart des Pragmatismus* (Berlin: Suhrkamp, 2013), pp. 97–120.

2 This book will not discuss skepticism, though; I am referring to it only as an example. See Hilary Putnam, *Reason, Truth and History* (Cambridge: Cambridge University Press, 1981), chapter 1, for a famous and controversial attempt to show that the thesis that we are 'Brains in a Vat' is necessarily false. Even according to that argument, the skeptical thesis is not meaningless.

3 For a rich set of different views by leading contemporary pragmatism scholars, see a collection I recently edited: Sami Pihlström (ed.), *The Continuum Companion to Pragmatism* (London and New York: Continuum/ Bloomsbury, 2011). On the pragmatic method in particular, see F. Thomas Burke, *What Pragmatism Was* (Bloomington: Indiana University Press, 2013).

4 I would again like to acknowledge Marcus Willaschek's influence on my arriving at this particular formulation, which I believe also leads us to reconsider the way in which James can be seen as a profoundly Kantian thinker. (See Chapter 2 for further details.)

5 See, for further elaboration, Sami Pihlström, *Pragmatist Metaphysics: An Essay on the Ethical Grounds of Ontology* (London and New York: Continuum, 2009); cf. also, for a somewhat different perspective, Willaschek, 'Bedingtes Vertrauen'. For a classical existentialist statement of how negativity and non-being yield an entanglement of metaphysical, ethical, and 'spiritual' concerns, see Paul Tillich, *The Courage to Be*, 2nd edn (New Haven, CT and London: Yale University Press, 2000; 1st edn 1952). Tillich insightfully reminds us about the significance of non-being for philosophy and theology.

6 The most important reference here is Peirce's best-known essay, 'The Fixation of Belief' (1877), available in, for example, *The Essential Peirce*, vol. 1, ed. Nathan Houser et al. (Bloomington and Indianapolis: Indiana University Press, 1992). Also the important anti-Cartesian writings from the late 1860s, including 'Some Consequences of Four Incapacities' (1868), can be found in the same volume.

DOI: 10.1057/9781137412669.0003

7   In addition to Peirce, the most important classical pragmatist from the point of view of the theory of inquiry is, obviously, Dewey. See especially John Dewey, *Logic: The Theory of Inquiry* (1938), available in Jo Ann Boydston (ed.), *The Collected Works of John Dewey: The Later Works*, vol. 12 (Carbondale: Southern Illinois University Press, 1986).

8   This conception of habituality has also been emphasized by pragmatist social theorists, including most famously Hans Joas but also other scholars, for example, in the Scandinavian context. See, for instance, papers by Erkki Kilpinen and Antti Gronow available at the website of the Nordic Pragmatism Network, www.nordprag.org (which contains numerous useful links to material on pragmatism). Kilpinen's major work on this topic is Erkki Kilpinen, *The Enormous Fly-Wheel of Society: Pragmatism's Habitual Conception of Rationality and Social Theory* (Helsinki: University of Helsinki, Department of Sociology, 2000).

9   See Dewey, *Logic*, as well as many other works by Dewey, available in his *Collected Works*.

10   'Real things' in this Peircean sense could also be humanly created objects and structures, as of course is the case in social-scientific inquiry. This is not the place to inquire into the ways in which (Peircean) pragmatism can or cannot embrace scientific realism. (I have explored this issue since the mid-1990s, and in my view it still remains open.) On 'real generals' in Peirce, see Chapter 1.

11   See Wittgenstein's famous discussion of family resemblances in *Philosophical Investigations*, trans. G.E.M. Anscombe (Oxford: Basil Blackwell, 1953; 2nd edn 1958), especially Part I, §§ 65–71.

12   It might be particularly problematic to apply the Peircean 'final opinion' account of truth to such areas of inquiry. Still we would hardly like to say that they have nothing at all to do with the concept of truth or that truth would simply be irrelevant in such fields. Here as elsewhere, pragmatism generally seeks to offer a balanced middle ground view.

13   Here my conception of inquiry represents a somewhat more liberal pragmatism than Peirce's – or, say, Cheryl Misak's; see her discussion of inquiry as necessarily pursuing truth in Misak, *The American Pragmatists* (Oxford and New York: Oxford University Press, 2013).

14   In the philosophy of religion, it is crucially important to understand that religion is very different from science – religious beliefs are not scientific theories or hypotheses – while not sliding all the way to the other extreme according to which rational considerations or criticism play no role whatsoever in the evaluation of religious ways of thinking and living. For a pragmatist attempt to find this balance, see Sami Pihlström, *Pragmatic Pluralism and the Problem of God* (New York: Fordham University Press, 2013). Note, however, that a 'religious inquiry,' pragmatically understood, may very well lead to a *loss* of one's religious identity. (Again, if it couldn't, it wouldn't be an inquiry.)

DOI: 10.1057/9781137412669.0003

1

Evil and Negativity: Sharpening the Pragmatic Method

Abstract: *This chapter explains why the approach through 'negativities' is important in ethical inquiry and how this follows and 'sharpens' the pragmatic method briefly discussed in the Introduction. Hence, this chapter deepens the very preliminary discussions of the introductory chapter. The concept of evil is also explored. An analysis of evil in terms of Charles Peirce's doctrine of 'real generals' is offered. It is also argued that 'theodicist' views, according to which the reality of evil can somehow, either theologically or secularly, be justified, are ethically unacceptable.*

Keywords: evil; negativity; limits; the pragmatic method; real generals; theodicy; anti-theodicy

Pihlström, Sami. *Taking Evil Seriously.* Basingstoke: Palgrave Macmillan, 2014. DOI: 10.1057/9781137412669.0004.

DOI: 10.1057/9781137412669.0004

Moral philosophy has, since antiquity, been understood as an examination of the good life,[1] while metaphysics, another key area of philosophical inquiry, has been regarded as a theoretical study of what exists or what is real at a basic or fundamental level (or what existence, reality, and related concepts mean). These fields of inquiry have thus been considered 'positively oriented' in the sense that they seek to characterize how goodness or existence (or related concepts) function in our thought or worldview(s), and which phenomena fall under these (or related) 'positive' concepts. As already preliminarily indicated in the introductory chapter, I will, contrary to this received view, argue that we should approach the kind of fundamental issues in philosophy that fields like ethics and metaphysics have been thought to address – and related issues of individual and social life, to the extent that philosophy is expected to be relevant to human life – *not primarily in terms of what is 'positively' real or good but 'through negation.'* Our primary conceptual orientation in these inquiries should be sought from finitude, non-existence, evil, and other negative notions. This *via negativa* methodology, as it might be labelled, can serve both metaphysical and ethical purposes, with applications in other fields of philosophy, including philosophy of religion.

For example, it can be argued that (human) life is best understood in terms of, or by paying close attention to, death; (moral) goodness in terms of evil; moral responsibility in terms of guilt and remorse; health in terms of illness, and more generally normality in terms of abnormality; happiness in terms of sorrow or grief; and existence (or presence) in terms of non-existence, loss, negativity, emptiness, or absence. Similarly, central human practices such as science and religion can be philosophically illuminated by drawing attention to their *corrupt* forms, such as pseudo-science or superstition or, possibly, to what happens in a *loss* of one's religious convictions. Furthermore, moral action and agency can be approached through a certain kind of *passivity*, that is, focusing not only on our capacity to act but also on what can be called 'moral vision,' the capacity to perceive some facts or events as ethically relevant, even if there is very little we can do about them (for example, because they are temporally/historically or geographically distant). Taking such moral passivity seriously entails that we view morality not only as a matter of action or acts but also as a matter of seeking the right or proper kind of attitude to what goes on around us. All these phenomena are, furthermore, cases of human *limits* and *finitude*. They lead us to acknowledge

DOI: 10.1057/9781137412669.0004

that there are many things between the heaven and the earth to which our actions and 'difference-making' powers do *not* reach.[2]

The philosophical literature on 'negative' topics such as evil and death has been growing over the past decade or two, with leading thinkers such as Richard Bernstein and Mark Johnston devoting volumes to such topics.[3] The systematic connections between the metaphysical and ethical dimensions of negativity in terms of their existential significance have not been worked out, however. This is what I propose to do through broadly Jamesian pragmatism. I will also argue that our negative approach in moral philosophy leads to an understanding of human beings' place in the world that might be described as 'melancholic,' or an understanding that acknowledges the 'tragic sense of life.'

The negative task of pragmatist philosophy

Don't get me wrong. As pointed out in the introduction, I am, of course, not saying that a field like anthropology which is concerned with the different ways people live in different cultures and societies should not study, comparatively, the different notions of goodness, or the good life. Anthropology is largely about people's ideas concerning what makes human lives good and about how people in different cultural contexts behave in relation to those ideas. There is no universally accepted content to the notion of 'the good life.' Not only according to cultural anthropology but also according to classical pragmatist philosophy of life, there is no universal key to the good life. Rather, there is an irreducible plurality of conceptions of the good life, both within and across human traditions and other commitments. Accordingly, our philosophy of (the good) life must be deeply pluralistic, in order to avoid being dogmatic, suppressive, and discriminatory.

However, it does not follow from the mere denial of, say, Aristotelian essentialism about *eudaimonia* and the denial of teleology generally that *philosophers* (as distinguished from anthropologists) should primarily explore comparatively different conceptions of the good (though, again, don't take me wrong by supposing that I would propose any clear division of labor between philosophy and anthropology). My approach in this entire book can, I suppose, be legitimately regarded as 'philosophical anthropology,'[4] but my basic point is that philosophy should consider the world, human beings, and human beings' thoughts about the world

DOI: 10.1057/9781137412669.0004

primarily from the point of view of negative concepts such as evil. More precisely, what I am saying is that philosophy should *focus* on such negative concepts. This is not to say that philosophy should be restricted to them, or to claim that goodness is unimportant or trivial – of course it isn't. Obviously, philosophy should continue to address 'the good life'; I am merely suggesting that turning attention to evil is a necessary – and certainly not sufficient – element of this project, if it is to be seriously carried out in the world we live in.

In this sense, I am drawing attention to what may be regarded as a necessary condition for a philosophical inquiry into goodness or the good life. Far from denying the importance of such inquiry in ethics – indeed, ethics could be *defined* as a field of philosophy investigating the good life – I am hoping to illuminate the philosophical context it needs to be successful or even possible. Hence, my argument for the priority of evil to goodness should not be taken to presuppose any binary opposition or essentialistic dichotomy between these notions. Clearly, there are also forms of ethical inquiry that work with concepts falling in between the two poles.[5] For instance, examining basic human needs and capabilities may lead to either a positive theory of human flourishing (where flourishing refers to a situation in which basic needs are satisfied and relevant capabilities are in maximal use) or a more negative theory of what happens when those needs fail to be satisfied. The latter, I claim, is necessary for developing the former, but the former may not be necessary for developing the latter. Even Aristotelian virtue ethicists need to pay attention to what happens, or may happen, when the virtues are violated. And conversely, as Albert Camus noted in a talk given in 1946, immediately after World War II, by saying *no* to the absurdity of the world and the 'civilization of death,' we are actually saying *yes* to human life, hope, and struggle.[6] In this sense, all my reflections on evil are also (I hope) ultimately in the service of the good.

In more than one way, then, my focus on evil and other negativities is exactly that – a focus. Furthermore, I am not relying on any specific moral theory; rather, I am inquiring into the nature of ethics or of the moral point of view itself. Note that it does not follow from the reasonable pragmatic anthropological pluralism about the good that our conceptions of 'the negative' – of evil and suffering, in particular – should or even could be as pluralistic and interpretation- and conceptualization-dependent as our conceptions of the good inevitably are. Rather, evil is the *shocking* reality taking us beyond the plural schemes of the good, and

DOI: 10.1057/9781137412669.0004

here lies its 'metaethical' significance (although I should also note that I am opposed to a dichotomy between metaethics and normative ethics; this inquiry should not be directly categorized as exclusively belonging to either). There is a sense in which *nothing is more real* than the suffering of the innocent victims of the concentration camps of the twentieth century.[7] On the other hand, there is no universal evil, either; evil itself takes many forms and spreads to ever new areas, like a fungus.[8] Yet, evil, as will be suggested later in this chapter, is something *general*. It also shows us a reality more robust than the varying and relative conceptions of goodness. It is only against a full recognition of this dark and tragic background of life, a recognition that must wear a human face, that our conceptions of the good can shine brightly.

Nor am I saying that any (moral) philosophy of evil should or even could offer a final, absolute definition of the concept of evil ('the essence of evil,' as it were), or adopt an ahistorical point of view on historical evils, or solve the theological problem of evil (the 'theodicy' problem), or neglect the anthropological, historical, political, and many other empirical particularities of evil. Yet, a philosophy of evil in our times may reflect on evil drawing both from classical philosophical works (for example, Kant's *Religionsschrift*, which contains Kant's theory of 'radical evil') and more modern ones (for example, Hannah Arendt's *Eichmann in Jerusalem*, which introduces the famous 'banality of evil'), together with any relevant empirical work on the psychology, sociology, and history of evil.[9]

Certainly I am not alone, or the first, in defending these ideas. Avishai Margalit argues in his rightly acclaimed book, *The Ethics of Memory* (2002), that we should focus on what he calls 'negative politics,' seeking to examine those phenomena (for example, humiliation) that threaten to collapse the entire moral community. (The analogy, of course, is negative theology, which is supposed to lead us to, or closer to, God by refusing to attach any positive predicates to God at all.) We need negative politics because we often 'recognize what is wrong with something without having a clear idea, or any idea at all, about what is right with it.'[10] This, I take it, is right on the mark. Negative politics, however, is needed not for its own sake but for the sake of a 'politics of dignity.' This kind of politics addresses, negatively, not how institutions can promote dignity – they can obviously do so in many ways – but rather 'how to stop humiliation,' that is, how to get rid of violations of dignity.[11] The 'positive' notion of dignity itself has little genuinely positive content, and the same holds for

DOI: 10.1057/9781137412669.0004

the notion of the good. Moreover, I believe Margalit is deeply right when he adds that 'we recognize dignity by the way we react to humiliation.'[12] Therefore, more generally, I am happy to join Margalit's proposal to focus on negativity:

> I opt to stress negative emotions – say, humiliation rather than pride, rejection rather than being recognized and accepted [...] as a strategy. The difference between dwelling on humiliation and not on recognition is not the same sort of difference as that between seeing the cup half empty and seeing it half full. The difference, I believe, cuts deeper. Is it not injustice rather than justice that 'hurts us into politics'? And tyranny rather than freedom, poverty rather than equality, humiliation rather than dignity?[13]

It is, I think, precisely the crisis, the melancholy, the evil, the suffering – you can add your favorite concepts – that hurt us into moral philosophy, and perhaps philosophy generally.[14] What interests us here is how the very search for the good life, or the moral project itself, may become endangered and threatened. These dangers and threats may be external, as we know from historical cases of evil inflicted on innocent human beings, but they may also be internal: the moral thinker her-/himself may be led to an existential nihilism that no appeals to the good life will ever be able to cure. There are forms of evil that may fragment the entire moral community we live in, and there are ways of experiencing evil that may make us think of the entire moral perspective as illusory. There are, moreover, philosophical and theological ways of reacting to evil that are themselves failures of recognition (in Margalit's sense), that is, do not adequately acknowledge the meaninglessness of suffering – as we will see in due course.

One of the main novelties of my approach to these issues is methodological, because a key method of my inquiry is the *pragmatic method*, developed in the late nineteenth century by Peirce and James, later further elaborated by other pragmatists like Dewey, and their followers (see the 'Introduction' above). It is, originally, a method of 'making our ideas clear' in terms of the potential or conceivable practical effects of their objects. I will argue that this pragmatic method can and should itself be developed into a 'negative' search for *minimal* (instead of maximal) conditions of, for example, morality. The practical 'difference' that our commitment to the moral point of view makes is that we will seek to meet certain minimal requirements of acceptable life, that is, to avoid humiliating others, rather than seeking to realize some positive and always culturally relative ideal of

DOI: 10.1057/9781137412669.0004

human flourishing. The relevant practical difference is not, or at least not primarily, a search for some positively characterized, or maximal, form of human flourishing.

In brief, it could thus be argued – such an argument itself being part of our moral reflection on good and evil – that one must primarily avoid being evil instead of (vaguely) seeking to be good. The former is already a major challenge we almost inevitably fail to meet. It may even be *dangerous* to focus too much on the good: monistic conceptions of the good may, for instance, be thought to legitimize war and aggression, at least when their cultural relativity is forgotten.[15]

Analogously in metaphysics: seeking minimal conditions of existence or reality (which I am *not* assuming to mean the same), we need to inquire into the nature of non-existence or unreality. While the ontological method of identifying minimal truthmakers, for example, is helpful here, its advocates, such as D.M. Armstrong, argue against metaphysical 'negativities.'[16] These arguments need critical analysis, because negativity, far from merely supervening on positive existence, can be seen as a key to ontological categorization itself: if something exists (or can exist), it is *not* (and cannot be) anything else than what it is. This can be explored as a logical and metaphysical principle, and it has obvious ethical relevance: when something is done, something else is *not* done; or, more precisely, no other action can take place in exactly the same spatio-temporal circumstances.

The pragmatic method can also be used to distinguish genuine and responsible inquiries into evil, death, and non-existence (and other negative concepts) from various pseudo-inquiries, including dogmatisms and fundamentalisms of different kinds. The epistemic willingness to *give up* one's convictions – even one's most deeply held beliefs – is itself a 'negativity,' a willingness to deliberately suffer loss. This requires continuous self-critical *reflexivity*, which joins the pragmatic method with another traditional philosophical method, the *transcendental method* originally developed by Immanuel Kant. Accordingly, a metaphilosophical goal of the present chapter is the critical reconciliation or integration of these two apparently very different philosophical methodologies, the pragmatist and the transcendental one, in the area of 'negative' inquiry into evil.[17] Hence, I hope to develop a novel integration of transcendental and pragmatist methodologies, and particularly applications of such an integration to the challenge of understanding ethical (and, by extension, metaphysical) negativities.

DOI: 10.1057/9781137412669.0004

Moreover, the rearticulation of the transcendental method may be employed to produce a novel account of a key concept of this methodology, the *transcendental self* (transcendental subjectivity), which must itself be understood as a kind of emptiness or absence (that is, 'nothing,' comparable to Jean-Paul Sartre's phenomenological analysis of consciousness) – or, as Ludwig Wittgenstein puts it in the *Tractatus* (1921), as a 'limit of the world' rather than a thing *in* the world. The transcendental subject in Wittgenstein's analysis makes the world possible instead of being an element to be found within it.[18] Accordingly, metaphysical and ethical issues can be approached from the point of view of the transcendental features of subjectivity, inquiring into how the world as a realm of objects as well as our relations to other subjects are so much as possible for us. Through such an inquiry, it is possible to investigate the necessary conditions ('transcendental conditions') for the possibility of phenomena assumed to be actual. Negativities like mortality and guilt may be among the conditions that make positive phenomena such as moral responsibility possible and constitute limits to their humanly possible forms. In this sense, even though I must leave the implications of my ideas to the understanding and rearticulation of transcendental subjectivity mostly implicit here (hoping to devote a separate essay to this topic), the present contribution is as much about the *concept of the moral self* – transcendentally and pragmatically conceived – as it is about evil.

William James's pragmatism offers one of the most important perspectives we should continue to develop on the issues of *self and otherness*, thus exploring the limits of individual ethical subjectivity. From the perspective of the kind of 'negative thinking' characterized above, our relations to other human beings must, once again, be reflected on not in terms of how we *succeed* in relating to them ethically, politically, or metaphysically (as if we could, for example, theoretically solve the 'problem of other minds'), but in terms of how we *fail* to do so. Here, again, the *via negativa* is the true pragmatic method of investigating how something (a view or conception, or a way of thinking and acting) 'makes a difference' in contrast to failing to do so. More generally, we should investigate our successes by focusing on our (actual and possible) *failures*. Negativity, instead of positivity, leads to deepened understanding: we can, as suggested above, appreciate the 'positive' requirements of morality by focusing on evil, that is, on what it is to fail to meet those requirements. Hence, our relation to others must be studied by beginning with James's

DOI: 10.1057/9781137412669.0004

important, though often neglected, metaphors of failures of connecting with others: our being 'deaf to the cries of the wounded' and 'a certain blindness in human beings.'[19] These metaphors refer to ways in which we fail in our attempts to encounter, meet, or relate to others; as Stanley Cavell and Hilary Putnam have suggested in a different context, the 'non-acknowledgment' of others is a pervasive human possibility.[20]

From these ordinary, everyday failures and inabilities of appropriate acknowledgment, we may derive a set of more theoretical philosophical issues, to which Jamesian pragmatism may offer considerable new articulations. The nature of evil itself is, obviously, one of these topics that need constant attention: we must take seriously, both ethically and metaphysically, the reality of evil in the world we live in – instead of constructing theodicies that explain evil away or seek to justify it.[21] James also leads us to new insights into the problem of other minds: we may be unable to 'make sense' – metaphysically, experientially, and conceptually – of there being, or even of the possibility of there being, other subjects of experience: the theoretical problem of solipsism (and 'other minds') derives from our failure of moral and metaphysical 'vision' (that is, our 'blindness' and 'deafness'). Regarding these and related issues, Jamesian pragmatism is fundamentally melancholic, hence 'negative'; the themes of evil and non-acknowledgment, we may argue, constitute a crucial link between James's religious investigations (especially *The Varieties of Religious Experience*, 1902) and his pragmatism (for example, *Pragmatism*, 1907).[22] Our fundamental relation to others is through (potential) failure of acknowledgment and the resulting guilt; there is no way to eliminate the permanent possibility of non-acknowledgment. Moreover, it is James's pragmatic method itself that leads us to understand our relation to otherness in terms of possible failure; this is the 'practical difference' our concepts of otherness, or their objects, make in our lives.

Moving briefly back to metaphysics again, James has, furthermore, been interpreted (for example, by Jose Medina) as defending a *relational conception of identity*, including the relationality of the identities of persons.[23] Part of our understanding of the strength and significance of 'negative thinking' is the realization that we need to ethically problematize our own ('positive') identity, or our own place in the world – that is, our very existence as the individual subjects we take ourselves to be. An individual needs and must use others, even the world generally; on the other hand, we also continuously give parts of ourselves to others. Thus, we both use others' losses for our own purposes and go through

DOI: 10.1057/9781137412669.0004

inevitable losses ourselves. Arguably, there is no stable, either Aristotelian or Cartesian, substantial identity that would remain the same through these processes – and this is what James's relational conception of identity may teach us. We therefore have to learn to think about our identities and moral existence through negation; yet, the ultimate result of such rethinking is a positive idea of an irreducibly moral relation to others: we are always already embedded in a network or field of moral relations, and we do not even exist (*qua* the individuals we are) independently of such relations. This is at the same time a challenge and an achievement: we do give parts of ourselves to others but cannot avoid failing to acknowledge, and even destroying, otherness around us. This makes moral existence, and hence human existence generally, *tragic*.

The ethical grounds of metaphysics are, then, highlighted here: if our moral existence is tragic, then our existence, generally, is tragic – though we will see in Chapter 2 that it may in the end be more advisable to use the concept of melancholy than the one of tragedy in this context.

A real general: toward a Peircean theory of evil

As suggested above and as will be further argued in Chapter 2, from James we may learn an ethically proper attitude to evil. But we may not learn much about what evil *is*. Well, perhaps we *shouldn't*. Evil is an open, irreducible, inscrutable category (as we may learn from other pragmatists, especially Richard Bernstein). But there is something slightly more metaphysical to say, and that is why I am now turning, for a moment, to another classical pragmatist, Charles Peirce. The Jamesian position (to be further developed throughout this chapter) needs to be supplemented by a Peircean one especially regarding the *generality* of evil.

Peirce himself wrote little on the problem of evil, theologically conceived.[24] I want to argue, however, that the Kantian doctrine of 'radical evil,' emphasizing our general *tendency* (*Hang*) to prioritize maxims that contradict the requirements of the moral law, needs something like a Peircean conception of real generals, because arguably we may be radically evil in the Kantian sense even if we never *in fact* act against the moral law (the categorical imperative).[25] Such potentially far-reaching practical consequences of Peircean pragmatic realism still remain insufficiently explored. Peirce was hardly a theorist of evil, but his realism

DOI: 10.1057/9781137412669.0004

about real generals[26] could be employed in an attempt to argue that evil itself is by its nature something general, irreducible to its practical instantiations – which clearly does not mean that we should postulate any 'entity-like' particularity in evil.

Approaching evil in this Peircean way is also, again, a way of applying the basic ideas of 'negative thinking' to the topic of evil itself: it is crucial that *evil does not have any particular place in the world's scheme of things*; we cannot place or isolate it in any definite 'corner' of the world and then deal with it. It is nowhere in particular. Often we cannot even identify it as a specific entity or class of entities (or as a process either, for that matter). On the contrary, as a Peircean-like 'general,' it is potentially everywhere and anywhere in the human world. This could be compared to Bernstein's references to evil as a 'fungus,' taken from Arendt's discussion of the banality of evil.

While Peirce himself hardly had any elaborate theory of evil, he did, in, for example, the 1893 essay, 'Immortality in the Light of Synechism,'[27] speak about the 'metaphysics of wickedness' – which he contrasted with his own synechism (the doctrine of continuity) and scholastic realism (the doctrine of real generals). Here wickedness is related to our tendency to view ourselves as individuals full and complete as we are. Our thought is entangled with such a metaphysics of wickedness if we maintain that 'I am altogether myself, and not at all you.'[28] Accordingly, the rejection of nominalism is for Peirce of utmost ethical significance. (However, the tendency to think nominalistically – to be in the grip of wickedness – is itself a general tendency.)

Hoping to clarify the ways in which evil is and is not a threat to the general meaningfulness and comprehensibility of the world,[29] I want to emphasize a distinction familiar from the philosophy of the human sciences, namely, the one between *explanation* and *understanding*. Evil is, presumably, not an explanatory concept.[30] Yet, some human actions must be *described* (and hence interpreted and understood) as evil – lacking any other morally appropriate way of describing those actions. Hence, the denial that evil functions as an explanatory concept does not entail the denial of its interpretive value. For instance, attaching the label 'evil' to the perpetrators of the Holocaust, or to their actions, seems to be the only moral option available; employing this notion is a condition of – not explaining why the Holocaust took place but – understanding the nature of the deeds of the perpetrators, including their 'banality' in Arendt's sense.

DOI: 10.1057/9781137412669.0004

In some cases understanding an individual action or event in a correct or appropriate (morally appropriate!) manner may, then, presuppose that we describe, conceptualize, and categorize it under the description (vocabulary, discourse) of evil. This means that we place it in a certain ethical, historical, political, and possibly also theological context that makes it intelligible as the special kind of action or event it is. A description of something or someone as evil may even be something we morally speaking owe to the victims of that action or that person (which is obviously very different from explaining those actions or the agents' reasons for performing them, let alone 'explaining them away' as evil). After such a description or understanding of an action as evil (in its specific context) has been provided, the action can often also be explained, possibly in quite different ways, for instance, intentionally by employing something like the practical syllogism,[31] say, by referring to Adolf Eichmann's attempts to promote his career and his beliefs about the necessary means for achieving such goals, or causally by referring to psychopathologies or other merely causal and/or natural, hence unintentional, facts and processes.[32]

However, while we certainly *can* understand and even explain evil actions, often extremely well, evil also takes us to the very limit of understanding. As Susan Neiman argues in her profound book, *Evil in Modern Thought* (2002),[33] evil is a challenge to *comprehensibility in general*, not just to understanding individual actions, events, or people. Let us pursue this a bit further by connecting the challenge of comprehensibility (understanding) with the pursuit of *meaningfulness*, which also goes to the heart of Jamesian pragmatism.[34]

How, we may ask, *could* human life be experienced as meaningful? More precisely, given the unbelievable sufferings of our fellow human beings, and given our own unavoidable guilt in the face of that suffering,[35] how could our experiences of meaningfulness, or the significance we perhaps claim to construct through our lives, be anything but illusory? The universe does not seem to care for our aspirations; in particular, it could not care less for our search for meaning and comprehension. Is the concept of meaningfulness even coherently applicable to, say, the life of a person who non-self-deceptively recognizes that her/his fellow humans have gone through the Holocaust (not to talk about the victims themselves)? Can the process of constructing meaning in and through life even get started in such a life? It is, after all, *meaningless* evil and suffering that emerges as a fundamental challenge for the value of

DOI: 10.1057/9781137412669.0004

life, and hardly anyone can deny that the world as we know it is full of meaningless evil and suffering.[36] This is one way of saying that the world, as we limited humans experience it, seems to be fundamentally absurd, incomprehensible.

The search for meaning, including the attempts to overcome absurdity and to somehow understand and live with (meaningless) evil, is both metaphysical and ethical. As Neiman puts it, '[w]e ask about the point of making theoretical sense of the world when we cannot make sense of misery and terror.'[37] Do we have to (in her words) 'deny philosophy' – accepting the limits of not just philosophical but any rational or intellectual discourse in contrast to, say, religious discourse – if we take evil seriously, admitting that it cannot, and perhaps ethically should not, be theoretically analyzed?[38] These worries go to the heart of the problem of justifying any theoretical or intellectual attitude to the world. Yet, it is not merely the theoretical attempt to understand meaning and value that is threatened by evil. The fact (if it is a fact) that 'the world contains neither justice nor meaning' is a threat both to our acting in the world and to our understanding it.[39] Philosophy, according to Neiman, begins, and threatens to end, with questions about 'what the structure of the world must be like for us to think and act within it' (rather than beginning with theoretical skeptical issues that largely define our philosophical tradition).[40] Just like the problem of evil inseparably entangled with it, the problem of finding meaning is 'fundamentally a problem about the intelligibility of the world as a whole,' a problem presupposing a tight link between ethics and metaphysics.[41] It is twentieth-century evil, in particular, the evil of the concentration camps, that seems not only to render evil generally ultimately intractable and unintelligible but also to undermine 'the possibility of intellectual response itself,' challenging rational attempts to understand the world.[42]

Referring to *The Brothers Karamazov*, Neiman writes:

> Dostoevsky underlined the idea that the problem of evil is not just one more mystery. It is so central to our lives that if reason stumbles there, it must give way to faith. If you cannot understand why children are tortured, nothing else you understand really matters. But the very attempt to understand it requires at least accepting it as part of the world that must be investigated. Some hold even this much acceptance to be unacceptable. Thus the rejection of theodicy becomes the rejection of comprehension itself.[43]

This provides the tone for the criticism of theodicies (see below) upon which the argument of the present book largely depends. The problem

DOI: 10.1057/9781137412669.0004

of evil, understood not as a mere theological puzzle but as a deep and general human problem, is a real test case for any views that may be defended regarding the issue of meaning. If no meaning can be found in a world of evil and suffering, in a world in which children are led to gas chambers, then the only *ethically* acceptable reaction *might* be to give up the intellectual, rational search for meaning altogether (including philosophical discourse) – because any such search might be entangled with the project of theodicy. This recognition of the ethical limits of philosophical inquiry might, moreover, be the only decent way to live with one's inescapable guilt and shame of being human, with one's being, helplessly, part of a world in which children are tortured. But, again, such a move, which we might conceive as the Jamesian 'sick soul's' response to evil and suffering,[44] could also be ethically (and perhaps even religiously) challenged. One might, and perhaps even should, insist on the continuous need for rational, philosophical discussion, even about evil.

Therefore, it is not at all clear what an adequate philosophical or intellectual response to evil could and should be like. The possibility remains that someone might find *this* frustrating situation itself meaningful. That is, the fact that no final answers, substantial or methodological, to our worries about evil and meaningfulness have been or perhaps ever can be given might be taken to be among the potential sources of meaning. These might be fragile sources of meaning, though.

It should now be clearer, I hope, why the kind of conception of evil as a challenge to comprehensibility itself sketched here might be argued to need metaphysical elaboration in terms of Peirce's 'real generals' (scholastic realism), and why the same can be said about Kant's famous theory of evil as a tendency (*Hang*) to certain kinds of prioritizations of maxims: it is not any individual action by itself but the *general tendency* to adopt certain kinds of maxims, or (in more Peircean terms) habits of action, instead of others that is relevant. Even more clearly, it is not a thing but a general property that things or processes (for example, actions or people) may have. Evil, when connected with the issue of the comprehensibility of the world, is inevitably anchored in *modal* concepts, and in the ways in which certain concepts necessarily structure our moral lives and our ways of attempting to understand those lives.[45]

Evil is, then, 'general,' not particular. We are not just attempting to understand individual phenomena, actions, and agents, but generalities in which they are involved.[46] It is from this generality that the issue of the comprehensibility of the world also emerges, and is constantly challenged

DOI: 10.1057/9781137412669.0004

by evil. As a generality, evil is never exhausted by its actual instances. It is a human potentiality, a Peircean-like 'real possibility' for all of us, even when things seem to be fine. Therefore – and for many other reasons as well – we must in the next chapter turn to James and the sick soul.

What's wrong with theodicies?

However, before doing that I want to explain at a relatively general level what I think is deeply wrong in attempts to justify evil – whether these attempts are religious or theological theodicies or secularized reinterpretations of theodicy.

Even though I am not primarily focusing on the philosophy of religion in this book, in this section I hope to offer a brief *ethical criticism of contemporary philosophy of religion*, especially of the discussion concerning evil (and particularly theodicy) within that field. As we will see, this amounts to a critique of a certain kind of *existential inadequacy* of philosophy of religion. Developing this ethical perspective on what is going on, and what is going wrong, in the philosophy of religion focusing on the problem of evil is therefore my specific task in the rest of this chapter, before I will seek a very different way of dealing with evil, based on James's thought, in the next chapter. I should note that I am not primarily interested in how the problem itself ought to be finally resolved, because I am skeptical about the very idea of finally resolving it. I am much more interested in inquiring into how it should or can be ethically responsibly discussed. Accordingly, I am convinced that the philosophical and existential relevance of the problem of evil is significantly broader than some mainstream philosophers of religion would be willing to admit. On the other hand, it is precisely for that reason that we should take a look at how the problem has been discussed by philosophers of religion.

So what is the current situation in the discussion of evil in this field, and what are its most pressing difficulties? Very briefly, the problem of evil is the problem of reconciling God's omnipotence, omniscience, and absolute goodness with each other. These attributes – or the statements attributing them to God – seem to conflict, because either God is unable to eliminate all the empirically real evil there is (in which case he is not omnipotent); or he does not know about its existence (in which case he is not omniscient); or he is not wholly good because he fails to eliminate it even though he knows about it and could eliminate it. The premises

DOI: 10.1057/9781137412669.0004

needed for the argument are, first, a relatively standard conception of the divinity attributing the above-listed properties to God and, second, the empirical premise that there is (unnecessary) evil in the world. Formally, the argument could be presented thus: (1) Necessarily, x is God if, and only if, x is omnipotent, omniscient, and absolutely good, and there is only one individual x such that x is God; (2) God would prevent or eliminate unnecessary evil; (3) there is unnecessary evil; (4) therefore, there is no God.

The problem of evil has traditionally been invoked as an 'atheological' argument, either in a logical or in an evidential form, by several critics of theism, including J.L. Mackie, Kai Nielsen, and William Rowe. In short, the *logical* version of the problem argues from the incompatibility of the key attributes of God with the empirical reality of evil to the non-existence of God. Theism, at least in the traditional sense, is taken to be logically incompatible with the reality of evil. Hence, atheism, or at least non-theism (including agnosticism), is claimed to follow deductively from the premises. In contrast, the *evidential* version makes the slightly more moderate point that it is a major theoretical burden of proof for the theist to reconcile the reality of evil with the co-presence of God's key attributes. That is, while the argument is not presented as a straightforward logical refutation of theism, it is suggested that the theist owes us an explanation of how the divine attributes are compatible with the existence of evil as we know it; thus, the empirical reality of evil is a major piece of evidence against theism.[47]

Here, however, we are not primarily concerned with these atheological uses of the argument, which can be argued to be problematic on independent grounds. The major problem with such arguments is that they presuppose an *evidentialist* understanding of religious beliefs. Evidentialists tend to view theism as a hypothesis comparable to scientific hypotheses that need to be evaluated in terms of available evidence. The reality of evil is then presented as a powerful set of evidence that speaks against theism. Evidentialism is a widespread background assumption for the testing and evaluation of philosophical and theological views on theism and evil. It is, however, an assumption we need not share; in any event, a proper understanding of the literature on the problem of evil requires that we see the various theodicies and 'defenses' that have been offered by authors such as Richard Swinburne, Alvin Plantinga, Peter van Inwagen, and others as working on the assumption of evidentialism (broadly conceived).[48]

DOI: 10.1057/9781137412669.0004

Another typical philosophical assumption shared by authors engaged in producing theodicies and defenses is a form of theological and/or religious *realism* that views realism in these fields as analogous to scientific realism. According to such a realistic picture, theology and philosophy of religion are in the business of constructing true theories that ideally correspond to the way the world is (and in less ideal circumstances at least approximate the mind-independent truth of the matter). This chapter, or book, is not a proper place to criticize realism in general.[49] However, it should be noted that not all philosophers of religion share the realistic understanding of the relation between philosophico-theological theorization and mind-independent (divine) reality. In contrast to strong realism, some philosophers of religion may argue that an adequate philosophical reaction to the problem of evil in particular is personal response and engagement instead of impersonal intellectual theory-construction. Such philosophers would generally resist invoking, say, God's 'reasons' for allowing evil as a theoretical concept that could do some explanatory work in the construction of a philosophical theory of evil (and theodicy), or conceiving of evil itself as a theoretico-explanatory notion.[50]

Here I will not be able to evaluate major background assumptions like evidentialism and realism in relation to the problem of evil. We just have to be conscious of them, and we have to understand that philosophers rejecting, for example, strong forms of realism (metaphysical realism), such as pragmatists following James, may develop quite different versions of realism (for example, 'pragmatic realism') in order to engage with the problem of evil.[51] The general point here, then, is that the relevant kind of realism invoked here need not be understood in terms of the analogy to scientific realism, as it often is understood. Such analogies may often be highly misleading. We will, in any event, revisit the issue of realism (at least implicitly) throughout this chapter when dealing with the need to recognize, or acknowledge, the *full reality* of evil and suffering.

Theistic thinkers have throughout centuries proposed theoretical responses to their (actual or imagined) opponents challenging theism by invoking the reality of evil. For example, Swinburne has argued for decades for a theodicy according to which a 'half-finished' universe that contains evil is the price we have to pay for the fact of human freedom. It is better that there are free agents in a world with evil than it would be if there were a world with neither evil nor freedom. More elaborate versions of this 'free will theodicy' have been defended by Plantinga and other leading 'reformed epistemologists' and other Christian philosophers.[52]

DOI: 10.1057/9781137412669.0004

Without going into any details, we may say that these are all 'instrumentalist' theodicies in the sense heavily criticized by thinkers as different as D.Z. Phillips and Marilyn McCord Adams.[53] The reality of evil, in such theodicist rationalizations, plays an instrumental role as a necessary condition for something else that is, all things considered, an overall good. In this sense, the reality of evil is not undermined or eliminated but is shown to play a necessary role in a supremely intelligent and benevolent God's cosmic project of universal salvation which crucially includes human freedom and which also renders existence ultimately meaningful. Something similar seems to happen in Peter van Inwagen's defense, which is one of the most impressive recent analytic achievements of theodicism. In his carefully argued volume, *The Problem of Evil*, van Inwagen emphasizes that he is *not* offering a theodicy but only a 'defense.' A theodicy and a defense need not differ in content; both are stories according to which both God and evil exist, but a theodicy is put forward as 'the real truth of the matter,' whereas a defense is, according to its author, a story that 'may or may not be true' but is argued to be consistent and epistemically possible.[54] In my terminology, a 'defense' of this kind may still belong, and typically does belong, to the *theodicist* tradition: the one who offers a defense – a story trying to make potential sense of God's allowing there to be evil – is still engaged in the process of *justifying* God's (possible) actions and (possible) reasons for them, even if s/he does not claim that the story told is true. The mere appeal to the epistemically possible here is justificatory in nature.

Moreover, the problem of evil for van Inwagen basically amounts to the problem of reconciling God's existence with the fact that there are 'bad things' in the world.[55] He refuses to recognize any *depth* in the concept of evil itself, as distinguished from (mere) badness. Furthermore, he notes that his task is 'a purely intellectual one,' a theoretical examination of the problem of evil understood as 'the problem that the real existence of bad things raises for theists.'[56] Thus, van Inwagen simply denies the 'intractability' or 'inscrutability' of evil emphasized by thinkers like Bernstein and Neiman.[57] For him the problem seems to be as transparent as any other conceptual and theoretical issue to be settled by using the powerful methods of analytic philosophy. It does not have any special mystery into it nor does it seem to be any more intimately connected with our human existence or the meaningfulness of our lives than any other intellectual issue.

DOI: 10.1057/9781137412669.0004

It is obviously very important for a philosopher to be explicit about the limitations of her/his approach and methodology. In this sense, I think van Inwagen's project is exemplary: he is very honest about what he is doing and what he is not doing, at least more explicit in this regard than many other mainstream analytic philosophers of religion. On the other hand, it is undeniable that he is not particularly sensitive to what some others have seen as the religious and existential depth of the problem, and of the corresponding religiously profound concept of evil. Not only does he set aside the Kantian-Arendtian concept of 'radical evil,' but he also rejects the idea that there is some 'overarching problem of evil' in the sense proposed by Neiman.[58] This is what he says:

> I am only a simple-minded analytical philosopher. [...] As I see matters, the problem of evil is what it has always been, a problem about God and evil. There is no larger, overarching problem of evil that manifests itself as a theological problem in one historical period and as a problem belonging to post-religious thought in another. I don't know how to argue for this conclusion, because I wouldn't know how to enter into anything I would call an argument with someone who would even consider denying it.[59]

Here, it seems to me, van Inwagen reveals the fundamentally *ahistorical* nature of his philosophical approach and methodology. His entire project becomes highly questionable as soon as we realize that when viewing religious ideas as responses to human problems naturally emerging within our lives, we are dealing with historically developing and reinterpretable matters.[60] While evil itself may be a persistent feature of human life, a fundamental experience that will be with us to stay, our interpretations of and responses to evil may take very different forms during the history of human thought and action. Theodicist responses, I am trying to argue, are unacceptable *for us*, in the historical situation we are now in, within the kind of practices we have developed. This is, in particular, something we may learn from post-Holocaust theorists of evil, including Arendt, Jonas, and Bernstein, for whom the Holocaust was not just one additional piece of evidence for the reality of evil and thus against theism but a turning point after which no human moral or intellectual categories can remain exactly what they were (see also Chapter 3).

In addition to developing a highly theoretical approach to the problem of evil and thereby manifesting insensitivity toward attempts to historicize either the problem itself or the relevant notion of evil, van Inwagen is even more strikingly insensitive toward what we may consider the ethical need to avoid overly intellectualized accounts of this problem.

DOI: 10.1057/9781137412669.0004

When suggesting that, 'for all logic can tell us, God might have reasons for allowing evil to exist that, in his mind, outweigh the desirability of the non-existence of evil,'[61] that God may have foreseen that 'free will is a sufficiently great good that its existence outweighs the evils that have resulted,'[62] that in the end it might happen that '[e]very evil done by the wicked to the innocent will have been avenged, and every tear will have been wiped away,'[63] and that, just as 'there can be cases in which it is morally permissible for an agent to permit an evil that agent could have prevented, despite the fact that no good is achieved by doing so,' this is 'the moral structure of the situation in which God finds himself when he contemplates the world of horrors that is the consequence of humanity's separation from him,'[64] van Inwagen engages in a theoretical speculation that might not only be considered insulting and even obscene by victims of evil but that may also be argued to be philosophically defective because of its failure to existentially *engage* human beings' problems – their experience of evil.

God's having *reasons* to allow evil – especially instrumental reasons that may outweigh some other considerations – makes God a calculating monster, as has been acknowledged by theodicists and anti-theodicists alike.[65] It is not primarily the argumentative structure carefully canvassed by van Inwagen that the anti-theodicist should be opposed to; it is, much more fundamentally, the picture he offers of the divinity and human beings' relations to both God and history that we should find simply ethically unacceptable. Van Inwagen points out that his account does explain why God might allow, and might have a reason to allow, evils happening to people 'without any reason,' because 'being separated from God' means to be 'the playthings of chance.'[66] *Therefore* people, including children, suffer and die horribly '*for no reason at all*.'[67] Yet, God has, according to van Inwagen's defense, reasons – and even good, ethically sound reasons – to allow *this* to be the case.

Just as van Inwagen says he finds it difficult to argue with those who claim to be able to grasp something like a comprehensive problem of evil (in Neiman's sense), I find it very difficult to provide any argumentative response to his 'defense' at this point. (This is also partly because I do not regard the problem of evil as an atheological argument in the first place.) I find it ethically disastrous – and, when it comes to one's possible theological pictures of the divinity, potentially blasphemous – to suggest that God might have 'good reasons' to allow the world he created to be a place in which children are led to gas chambers. If one's philosophical approach leads one to say things like that, then there is surely something wrong with that philosophical approach, rather than *vice versa*. One should not only recognize the limits of philosophical argumentation – the fact that we should *not* always follow the intellectually most sophisticated argument, wherever it leads[68] – but one should more generally be continuously aware of the ethical context(s) in which one's philosophizing takes place.

It is, arguably, part of this contextuality that philosophy should, in dealing with (as Dewey put it) 'problems of men,' also offer some kind of *comfort* to the suffering.[69] Now, van Inwagen is again quite conscious of the limitations of his approach, and this is to his merit. He says explicitly that he is not, in offering his defense, attempting to even hypothetically comfort anyone.[70] It is precisely for this reason that we may, and should, reject his 'defense' with the words James directed at Leibnizian theodicies, that is, as 'a cold literary exercise, whose cheerful substance even hell-fire does not warm.'[71] A philosophical reflection on the problem of evil should avoid the purely intellectual God's-Eye View adopted by van Inwagen and should sincerely acknowledge our human limits in dealing with this problem, maintaining sensitivity not only to the victims of evil but also to everyone needing comfort in the (historically developing) situation of having to live within such limits.

Our challenge in this chapter (and implicitly throughout the book), therefore, is to defend a resolutely anti-theodicist philosophy that will be more sensitive to the human dimensions of the problem of evil than van Inwagen's purely theoretical approach. In short, a pragmatist form of anti-theodicy ought to do the job of engaging and even comforting the victim, which van Inwagen's analytic approach is manifestly incapable of – not, of course, simply because it is a piece of analytic philosophy but because it lacks the kind of fundamental ethical orientation that critics of theodicies have in my view rightly asked for.

Anti-theodicism

Indeed, several thinkers have argued, against theodicisms of various kinds, that offering a theodicy – religious or secular – is a way of explaining away, and thereby justifying, the existence of evil and that this amounts to an ethically unacceptable, or even obscene, reaction to the evil and suffering that human beings, especially the victims of historical

DOI: 10.1057/9781137412669.0004

atrocities such as the Holocaust, have to go through in their lives. We must never, it can be argued, 'excuse' evil in this sense, nor should we speculate about the possible reasons that an omnipotent and benevolent God (if God existed) might have for allowing apparently unnecessary evil to exist, because such speculations would turn God into a monster. One of the most powerful anti-theodicist arguments in contemporary philosophy of religion has been provided by D.Z. Phillips, whose point of departure is Wittgensteinian philosophy of religion.[72]

Briefly, according to what we may call Wittgensteinian anti-theodicism,[73] the proper use of religious and/or theological language does not incorporate or even tolerate theodicies, or any speculations about God's possible reasons for allowing horrendous suffering. These issues should, rather, be addressed in properly religious and poetic language, such as the language we find in the Book of Job. Rationalizing theodicies make God himself an evil demon. No benevolent creator could just sit back and contemplate the beauty of his divine plan when something like the Holocaust is taking place among his creatures. The reasons for the rejection of theodicies are, hence, both ethical and religious (and, arguably, even aesthetic). Ethically, theodicies are *simply outrageous*,[74] disregarding the sufferings of the victims and demonstrating crude moral insensitivity to those unfortunate people who have (had) to go through such experiences. Theologically and religiously, theodicies are *conceptual confusions* in which we human beings hopelessly try to justify God's ways of thinking and acting which, if invoked at all, ought to be regarded as completely different from ours. Arguably, one should not undertake such a confused and possibly even blasphemous task if one wants to be 'genuinely religious' rather than pseudo-religious or superstitious.[75] Catastrophes, natural and moral, may strike us 'without rhyme or reason'; moralizing and intellectualizing speculations about why they happened should be discouraged. Rather, the proper response is silence and wonder, perhaps faith and prayer – but equally possibly also the *loss* of faith, depending decisively on the individual case.

Anti-theodicism is, however, not restricted to special paradigms in contemporary philosophy of religion such as the Wittgensteinian one. Clearly, there are anti-theodicist thinkers (who would typically not use these words) that find the very idea of excusing or explaining away evil morally unacceptable without caring too much about the theological confusions involved. These more secular anti-theodicists

DOI: 10.1057/9781137412669.0004

include philosophers writing in the tradition of Jewish responses to the Holocaust, such as Jonas and Bernstein, but also, arguably, philosophers coming from a quite different intellectual background, such as James (see further Chapter 3). An important literary contribution to anti-theodicist thinking is of course Dostoevsky's character Ivan Karamazov, who famously 'returns his ticket' to the God who (supposedly) created a world in which children are tortured.[76]

Now, while anti-theodicist argumentation is in my view compelling, both ethically and religiously (as this book as a whole will, I hope, contribute to demonstrating), it would be wrong to conclude that theod-icies are mere relics of the past. On the contrary, they flourish in ever more sophisticated forms in contemporary philosophy of religion. Not all theodicies are as insensitive to human suffering as (I have argued) van Inwagen's. Some of them oppose the 'instrumentalization' of evil and suffering in the service of some allegedly greater good, just like anti-theodicies do. A novel proposal in this discussion has been offered by Marilyn McCord Adams, a major authority in the field who again returns to the problem of evil in a recent article.[77] Let me conclude this chapter by discussing her proposal. The reason for exploring her position is that she is one of the few theodicy-seeking philosophers who take seriously the kind of anti-theodicist worries that play a key role in thinkers like Jonas, James, and Phillips.

Adams agrees with Phillips's criticism of 'instrumentalist' theodicies that finds '*morally obscene any idea that instrumental reasons could impose [...] moral obligation or confer [...] moral permission on and so wash the hands of agents who allow them.*'[78] Only philosophers who 'separate the theoretical problem of evil from the existential context in which horrors arise'[79] can come up with such ideas. This, precisely, is what philosophers like Swinburne, Plantinga, and van Inwagen seem to be doing. As I have argued above, van Inwagen's 'defense' is, in Jamesian terms, a 'cold liter-ary exercise' that 'even hellfire cannot warm.'

Rather, when we are not only suffering from evil but ourselves led to be involved in evil, as, famously, the protagonist in William Styron's *Sophie's Choice*, the evil is not and cannot be just excused because some other (possibly greater) evil is thereby avoided but remains with us, 'sticks with' us.[80] However, this does not mean, according to Adams, that we should not view God as 'an agent-cause' 'acting in our world.' What Adams offers is a picture of divine goodness that includes an idea

DOI: 10.1057/9781137412669.0004

of God as infinitely good in a rather heavily metaphysical sense. God is *not* 'a good for which horrors are instrumentally necessary,' and 'beatific intimacy' with the divinity is *not* 'a goal for the sake of which horrors are tolerated as the price' – that would, indeed, be cruel and obscene – but rather, 'as incommensurably good for the created person, beatific intimacy with God can overcome the *prima facie* life-ruinous quality of horror participation.'[81] Moreover, there is an element of 'divine solidarity' in God's own 'horror participation' due to the incarnation; in this sense this is a specifically Christian response to the problem of evil and suffering.

Thus, Adams maintains that insofar as we 'recognize our own horror participation as an episode of intimate togetherness in our – on the whole and in the end – beatific life together with God, we would not retrospectively wish it away from our life histories.'[82] Now this, I take it, is an extremely problematic thing to say. I believe it could still be found cruel and obscene from the point of view of, say, Holocaust survivors to appeal to *any* kind of compensation, even infinite post-mortem compensation. Could we, any one of us, console a Holocaust victim in this way? Could such a victim *avoid* wishing certain experiences away from her/his life history?[83]

Thinkers like Jonas and Bernstein would presumably answer these questions negatively (cf. Chapter 3). They would find it outrageous to suggest anything like this. I do not think this difference in opinion about such a fundamental matter can be reduced to the difference between Judaism and Christianity in this regard. It is a deep ethical difference in the ways we recognize other people.

The issue of *recognition*, then, could be regarded as a key to this entire problem.[84] Do we properly recognize a victim or a sufferer if we console her/him by invoking the idea of a post-mortem beatific intimacy? Adams recognizes (sic!) that Phillips, given his Wittgensteinian rejection of personal survival after death, cannot accept the idea that full recovery from horror participation takes place after death.[85] However, this is hardly the point. Much more importantly, our basic ethical recognition of another human being as a sufferer might require us not to talk about any 'full recovery' at all. Very simply, we owe to the victims, as part of our recognition of them, the recognition that there can be no 'full recovery' after an event like the Holocaust; indeed, it has famously been suggested that there can be no more poetry, art, philosophy, or

DOI: 10.1057/9781137412669.0004

even rational thought after the Holocaust. To claim that God, after our deaths, 'heals our meaning-making capacities', teaching us 'how to make positive sense of our lives',[86] can only sound like an incredible insult to anyone who really has to go through suffering of the magnitude of the Holocaust. Equally insulting is in my view Adams's claim that because of this supreme divine healing, 'even the Hitlers and Pol Pots of this world will eventually be able to live with themselves',[87] as horror participation can be posthumously healed as much in the case of the perpetrators as in the case of the victims.

It is, then, nothing short of unbelievable to hear someone seriously suggest that we will wear our sins 'eternally as honorable battle scars'.[88] Again, just try talking in this way about the sins of a Holocaust perpetrator to someone whose family was murdered at Auschwitz. The way we speak, our use of language, however banal, plays a fundamentally ethical role in our orientation toward other human beings, their experiences, and the world in general. Our next task is to look and see whether Jamesian pragmatism could help us in taking some steps toward an ethically appropriate way of relating to otherness.

Notes

1   As a classical version of this idea, just think of Aristotle's conception of happiness, *eudaimonia*, as the only thing pursued because of itself (while everything else is pursued instrumentally with happiness always being the final goal). See the opening of Aristotle's *Nicomachean Ethics*, Book 1, for the most famous formulation of this position (electronically available, for example, at the Perseus Project website, www.perseus. tufts.edu).

2   This *via negativa* argument has also been sketched regarding the specific case of guilt as a necessary condition for the possibility of morality in Sami Pihlström, *Transcendental Guilt: Reflections on Ethical Finitude* (Lanham, MD: Lexington Books / Rowman & Littlefield Publishing Group, 2011).

3   See, for example, Richard Bernstein, *Radical Evil: A Philosophical Interrogation* (Cambridge: Polity Press, 2002), and *The Abuse of Evil* (Cambridge: Polity Press, 2005); Mark Johnston, *Surviving Death* (Princeton, NJ: Princeton University Press, 2010).

4   Or, perhaps, 'philosophy of the human condition', if the phrase 'philosophical anthropology' sounds problematic. Cf. here Sami Pihlström, 'On the Possibility of Philosophical Anthropology', *Journal of Philosophical Research* 28 (2003b), 259–85.

DOI: 10.1057/9781137412669.0004

5   If we were phrasing this in terms of the distinction between the good and the bad, there would be more room for quantitative differences along one and the same scale. However, speaking about evil (in contrast to the merely 'bad') indicates a move to a qualitatively different level. In brief, we may allow that 'bad' is a quantitative concept whereas the concept of evil refers to something that challenges, or even threatens to destroy, the moral universe altogether, with whatever scales of good vs. bad it includes. In a way, we might say that it moves in the same conceptual space as the notion of 'moral perfectionism' made famous by Stanley Cavell in his readings of Emerson and Thoreau: see Cavell, *The Senses of Walden*, rev. edn (Chicago and London: University of Chicago Press, 1992; 1st edn 1971). While I of course acknowledge that moral perfectionism entails taking very seriously all kinds of imperfection, failure, and non-acknowledgment, I by no means subscribe to Cavell's position here.

6   Albert Camus, *Die Krise des Menschen* (originally 'La crise de l'homme,' a lecture delivered in New York in 1946, published in French in Camus's *Oeuvres completes*, 1965), available in German as a 'Sammelbeilage' of *Philosophie Magazin* 11 (2013).

7   This view will be discussed and further developed on the basis of Hans Jonas's post-Holocaust moral and religious philosophy in Chapter 3.

8   The fungus metaphor has been used by authors such as Hannah Arendt and Richard Bernstein, again as a response to the shock of the Holocaust. See Chapters 2 and 3.

9   Kant's *Religion innerhalb der blossen Vernunft* (1793–94) is available, for example, in Immanuel Kant, *Werke in zehn Bänden*, ed. Wilhelm Weischedel (Darmstadt: Wissenschaftliche Buchgesellschaft, 1983). Arendt's work on Eichmann is available, for example, in *The Portable Hannah Arendt* (New York: Viking, 2007). For influential empirical sociopsychological studies on the human capacity for evil, see, for example, Philip Zimbardo, *The Lucifer Effect: How Good People Turn Evil* (London: Rider, 2007); and Harald Welzer, *Täter: Wie aus ganz normalen Menschen Massenmörder werden* (Frankfurt am Main: Fischer, 2005; 3rd edn 2009).

10 Avishai Margalit, *The Ethics of Memory* (Cambridge, MA and London: Harvard University Press, 2002), p. 113.

11 Ibid., p. 114.

12 Ibid., p. 115.

13 Ibid., p. 112. We will return to recognition – and, negatively, to the lack of recognition – toward the end of this volume (see Chapter 4).

14 A strikingly similar picture of our fundamental starting point in philosophy is painted by Simon Critchley, who argues that philosophy begins from disappointment, from the realization of human finitude. See Critchley, *How to Stop Living and Start Worrying* (Cambridge: Polity, 2010), and Critchley, *Infinitely Demanding: Ethics of Commitment, Politics of Resistance*

(London: Verso, 2007; paperback edn, 2012). In the latter book, Critchley explicitly suggests that modern philosophy, starting from Kant's Copernican turn, 'begins in disappointment' in the sense that it is a lesson in human limitations (p. 1). What this means ethically is a (broadly Levinasian) insistence on the 'unfulfillability of the ethical demand,' leading to an 'ethics of discomfort' (Critchley, *Infinitely Demanding*, pp. 10–11). Critchley comes very close to the kind of negative thinking I am proposing here when he further says that the conception of the self as 'fundamentally an ethical subject' – that is, the close connection between ethics and the understanding of the self – is 'best argued negatively, through the experience of failure, betrayal and evil' (Critchley, *Infinitely Demanding*, pp. 20–1). What he does not address is the way in which pragmatism, for example, James's, might be an articulation of this *via negativa* method.

15   Works by theorists of evil such as Bernstein (see above) and Tzvetan Todorov – see Todorov, *Facing the Extreme: Moral Life in Concentration Camps* (New York: Metropolitan/Holt, 1996) – are worth mentioning here. Note that it may, admittedly, be dangerous to focus too much on evil as well. If our moral philosophy becomes too gloomy and pessimistic, this may undermine any moral hope and motivation we might still be capable of entertaining, which would lead to an utter loss of the moral drive, or of anything like what James called the 'strenuous mood.' Thus, I am certainly not recommending an *exclusive* focus on evil. What I am recommending is *taking evil seriously* even when we prefer to focus on the good.

16   See D.M. Armstrong, *Truth and Truthmakers* (Cambridge: Cambridge University Press, 2004).

17   This interpretation has more generally been one of my continuous endeavors since the late 1990s and early 2000s; cf., for example, Sami Pihlström, *Naturalizing the Transcendental: A Pragmatic View* (Amherst, NY: Prometheus/Humanity Books, 2003a), and Pihlström, *Pragmatist Metaphysics*.

18   Ludwig Wittgenstein, *Tractatus Logico-Philosophicus* (1921), trans. Brian McGuinness and David F. Pears (London: Routledge and Kegan Paul, 1974), §§ 5.6ff.

19   See, for example, William James, 'On a Certain Blindness in Human Beings,' in James, *Talks to Teachers on Psychology and to Students on Some of Life's Ideals* (1899); on the 'cries of the wounded' metaphor, see the famous essay, 'The Moral Philosopher and the Moral Life,' in James, *The Will to Believe and Other Essays in Popular Philosophy* (1897). Both volumes are available in *The Works of William James*, ed. Frederick H. Burkhardt, Fredson Bowers, and Ignas K. Skrupskelis (Cambridge, MA and London: Harvard University Press, 1983 and 1979, respectively).

20   Cf. Stanley Cavell, *The Claim of Reason* (Oxford: Oxford University Press, 1979); Hilary Putnam, *Philosophy in an Age of Science* (Cambridge, MA and London: Harvard University Press, 2012).

DOI: 10.1057/9781137412669.0004

21 Furthermore, the rationality of religious faith, one of James's major concerns, could be discussed in terms of the same *via negativa* method: the problem, for James, is not credulity but inability or failure to embrace faith, even given the pragmatic 'right' to believe (*contra* naïve readings of James's pragmatism as a defense of wishful thinking). This book, however, is not (centrally or primarily) a study on the philosophy of religion.

22 Both are available in *The Works of William James*, 1985 and 1975, respectively.

23 This interpretation by Medina will be briefly revisited in Chapter 3.

24 Cf., however, for example, W2:126–7. References to Peirce will be provided with the standard abridgments, with CP standing for Charles S. Peirce, *The Collected Papers of Charles Sanders Peirce*, 8 vols (Cambridge, MA: Harvard University Press, 1931–58), W for *The Writings of Charles S. Peirce*, 8 vols to date, The Peirce Edition Project (Bloomington and Indianapolis: Indiana University Press, 1980–), and EP for *The Essential Peirce*, 2 vols, The Peirce Edition Project (Bloomington and Indianapolis: Indiana University Press, 1992–98).

25 See Kant, *Religionsschrift*, chapter 1, for the theory of radical evil. We need not subscribe to Kant's account of the categorical imperative in order to find this notion useful (and open to a Peircean metaphysical backing).

26 On Peirce's 'scholastic realism' about generality, see several essays in EP2, as well as the comprehensive discussion, with ample references to secondary literature, in Pihlström, *Pragmatist Metaphysics*, chapter 6. Very briefly, Peirce's realism is a view according to which there are real generals like laws, habits, and dispositions, which are not reducible to existing particulars. Existence and reality need to be distinguished: while particulars exist (or fail to exist), generals are real, without existing.

27 EP2:1–3.

28 EP2:2.

29 Regarding evil and comprehensibility – and Peircean generality – I am here briefly returning to some considerations elaborated on in my previous book, *Pragmatic Pluralism and the Problem of God* (chapter 5).

30 Here, I think, we should agree with Philip Cole, *The Myth of Evil* (Edinburgh: Edinburgh University Press, 2006).

31 For a classical treatment, see Georg Henrik von Wright, *Explanation and Understanding* (Ithaca, NY: Cornell University Press, 1971).

32 One important background idea here might be Donald Davidson's theory of actions and events: some events can be described, hence understood, in a special way as intentional actions. The same events can be described and explained both in an intentional and in a causal vocabulary. See Davidson, *Essays on Actions and Events* (Oxford: Clarendon Press, 1980).

33 Susan Neiman, *Evil in Modern Thought: An Alternative History of Philosophy* (Princeton, NJ: Princeton University Press, 2002; paperback edn, 2004).

DOI: 10.1057/9781137412669.0004

34   The concepts of meaning and understanding are of course linked. When understanding something, that something must have a meaning which we understand. If we are able to 'understand' human life, or the world in which it takes place, that life (or world) must have some kind of meaning. One of James's most explicit treatments of this topic is his essay, 'Is Live Worth Living?', in *The Will to Believe*, in *The Works of William James* (1979); the theme is, however, important in almost everything he wrote.

35   See my *Transcendental Guilt*. Cf. here also Simon Critchley's remarks on guilt and original sin. What he says, coming very close to the ideas I am defending here, is that 'the phenomenon of guilty conscience reveals – negatively – the fundamentally moral articulation of the self' (*Infinitely Demanding*, p. 23). Guilt follows from the fact that the self is not 'equal' to its moral demands (see Critchley, *Infinitely Demanding*, p. 53). Theologically, or in our 'uneasy godlessness with a religious memory' (Critchley, *Infinitely Demanding*, p. 2), this translates into the notion of original sin, expressing the 'ontological defectiveness of the human being, that there is something essentially flawed about what it means to be human, [...] a lack that we cannot make up and whose origin goes back to our origin [...]' (Critchley, *How to Stop Living and Start Worrying*, pp. 44–5).

36   Evil and suffering intensify the problem of the meaningfulness of life but do not exhaust it, because mere *mortality* may be taken to deprive life of meaning. These problems are, of course, connected, as death itself can be, and has often been, regarded as evil, even though the contrary view, according to which immortality would be meaningless, has also been advanced. The present book does not directly address the issues of death and mortality; see, however, Jeff Malpas and Robert C. Solomon (eds.), *Death and Philosophy* (London and New York: Routledge, 1998), as well as Sami Pihlström, 'Death – Mine or the Other's? On the Possibility of Philosophical Thanatology', *Mortality* 6 (2001), 265–86. This is also a topic to which pragmatists should direct more attention. For a promising start, see Charles A. Hobbs, 'Why Classical American Pragmatism is Helpful for Thinking about Death', *Transactions of the Charles S. Peirce Society* 47 (2011), 182–95.

37   Neiman, *Evil in Modern Thought*, p. xviii.

38   See Ibid., p. 42. On the 'intractability' of evil, see again Bernstein, *Radical Evil* and *The Abuse of Evil*. Both Neiman's and Bernstein's books can be read as reminding us of the problem of evil as *the* challenge for any rational attempt to evaluate philosophically the meaningfulness of life.

39   Neiman, *Evil in Modern Thought*, p. 7.

40   Ibid., p. 5. Thus, Neiman's project, focusing on evil, is to lead philosophers back to the 'real roots of philosophical questioning' (Neiman, *Evil in Modern Thought*, p. 13), redescribing the tradition of modern philosophy as a struggle

DOI: 10.1057/9781137412669.0004

with the problem of evil (rather than, say, with the problem of external world skepticism). Note that this is precisely the understanding of the problem of evil, emphasizing that evil threatens our ability to regard the world as comprehensible, that conservative philosophers of religion, for example, Peter van Inwagen, firmly reject (see van Inwagen, *The Problem of Evil* [Oxford: Clarendon Press, 2006], pp. 15–16).

41   Neiman, *Evil in Modern Thought*, pp. 7–8. This link could be strengthened by following Wittgenstein in regarding the world and life as, ultimately, 'one.' See Wittgenstein, *Tractatus*, § 5.621; for a useful commentary regarding this matter, see Martin Stokhof, *World and Life as One: Ethics and Ontology in Wittgenstein's Early Philosophy* (Stanford, CA: Stanford University Press, 2002).

42   Neiman, *Evil in Modern Thought*, p. 256.

43   Ibid., p. 325.

44   I am of course referring to James's thematization of the sick soul in *The Varieties of Religious Experience*; see Chapter 2.

45   Guilt, 'transcendentally' analyzed, is a similar concept in this regard, though of course not the same concept. Cf. Pihlström, *Transcendental Guilt*. For a reminder of the fact that, despite our tendency to easily conform to evil, there are also individuals who are in real-life cases able to resist such tendencies and refuse to kill and destroy even when exposed to major social pressure, see Eyal Press, *Beautiful Souls: The Courage and Conscience of Ordinary People in Extraordinary Times* (New York: Picador, 2012).

46   A Peircean pragmatist may also adopt the concept of a *habit* here. Note, however, also that evil must not be *reduced* to generality (or Peirce's Thirdness). It also has the 'brute-factness' of what Peirce called Secondness and the qualitative immediacy of Firstness. All three Peircean categories are needed in an adequate pragmatist account of evil. For Peirce's category theory, see, for example, some of the key texts in *The Essential Peirce* (the early 1867 statement, 'On a New List of Categories,' is available in EP1, chapter 1).

47   See, for example, William Rowe (ed.), *God and the Problem of Evil* (Malden, MA and Oxford: Blackwell, 2001); Chad Meister, *Evil: A Guide for the Perplexed* (London: Bloomsbury, 2012).

48   For an overview of the problem of evil in the philosophy of religion, with a comprehensive bibliography listing most of the key contributions, see Michael Tooley, 'The Problem of Evil,' *Stanford Encyclopedia of Philosophy* (2012), http://plato.stanford.edu/entries/evil/.

49   See, however, my remarks (below) on a Jamesian-Feyerabendian response to the issue of realism.

50   Moreover, the attempts to develop theodicies seeking to justify the existence of evil might themselves be regarded as 'anti-realistic' in a quite different sense: such attempts would not take seriously the reality of evil as we know it but would rather swipe it under the carpet. Theodicies would not, then,

DOI: 10.1057/9781137412669.0004

maintain a truly 'realistic spirit' in their attempt to face evil. I am borrowing the notion of a 'realistic spirit' from Cora Diamond: see her *The Realistic Spirit* (Cambridge, MA and London: The MIT Press, 1991). For a brief discussion of this notion in relation to William James's philosophy of religion, see Sami Pihlström, 'Pragmatic Realism and Pluralism in Philosophy of Religion,' in Henrik Rydenfelt and Sami Pihlström (eds), *William James on Religion* (Basingstoke: Palgrave Macmillan, 2013).

51   My own approach in *Pragmatic Pluralism and the Problem of God* is an example of this.

52   Another version of what we may call 'theodicist' thinking today is the approach known as *skeptical theism*, according to which we cannot know God's reasons for allowing evil (or for many other things, including his – and his reasons' – hiddenness from us) but the theist may nevertheless trust, and perhaps justifiably believe, that there are such reasons unknown and perhaps unknowable to us. See Meister, *Evil: A Guide for the Perplexed*, for a discussion of the relation between the problem of evil and skeptical theism.

53   For an exchange between Swinburne (the theodicist) and Phillips (the anti-theodicist), see, for example, their contributions, both titled 'The Problem of Evil,' in Stuart C. Brown (ed.), *Reason and Religion* (Ithaca, NY and London: Cornell University Press, 1977), pp. 81–102 and 103–21, respectively. Swinburne and Phillips have continued to examine these topics voluminously after those early papers. However, their conflict – the paradigmatic opposition between theodicism and anti-theodicism – basically seems to repeat the old patterns of argument. I will get back to Adams's views in due course.

54   Van Inwagen, *The Problem of Evil*, p. 7.

55   Ibid., p. 4.

56   Ibid., p. 12.

57   See, again, Bernstein, *Radical Evil*; and Neiman, *Evil in Modern Thought*. There are also other recent theorists of evil who have insisted on the peculiar depth of the concept – retaining some of its traditional religious character in a secularized context. See, for example, Alan D. Schrift (ed.), *Modernity and the Problem of Evil* (Bloomington and Indianapolis: Indiana University Press, 2005); and Peter Dews, *The Idea of Evil* (Malden, MA: Blackwell, 2008).

58   Van Inwagen, *The Problem of Evil*, pp. 14–15. He admits that he has 'a very narrow conception of philosophy' in comparison to the one at work in Neiman's *Evil in Modern Thought*.

59   Van Inwagen, *The Problem of Evil*, p. 16.

60   I make this point more fully in Pihlström, *Pragmatic Pluralism and the Problem of God*, chapter 5 and 'Conclusion.'

61   Van Inwagen, *The Problem of Evil*, p. 65; see also p. 98.

62   Van Inwagen, *The Problem of Evil*, p. 72.

DOI: 10.1057/9781137412669.0004

63 Ibid., p. 89.

64 Ibid., p. 111.

65 See also Ibid., p. 145.

66 Van Inwagen, *The Problem of Evil*, p. 89.

67 Ibid. (original emphasis).

68 For critical discussions of this idea, see Sami Pihlström, *Pragmatism and Philosophical Anthropology: Understanding Our Human Life in a Human World* (New York: Peter Lang, 1998), chapter 10, as well as Pihlström, *Transcendental Guilt*, chapter 4.

69 This is, I believe, especially easy to accept if you are a philosopher with pragmatist leanings. Pragmatists like James and Dewey famously insisted that philosophy must be relevant to human beings' genuine problems, instead of just being theoretically and intellectually relevant. (On the other hand, there should, especially for pragmatists, be no fundamental dichotomy between 'theoretical' and 'practical' philosophy, or relevance.) For Dewey's views on the relevance of philosophy in investigating 'the problems of men,' see John Dewey, *The Problems of Men* (New York: Philosophical Library, 1946).

70 Van Inwagen, *The Problem of Evil*, p. 108.

71 James, *Pragmatism*, p. 20. See also, on James's specific version of anti-theodicism, Sami Pihlström, *'The Trail of the Human Serpent Is over Everything': Jamesian Reflections on Mind, World, and Religion* (Lanham, MD: University Press of America [Rowman & Littlefield Publishing Group], 2008), chapter 4. See further Chapter 2.

72 See again Phillips's response to Swinburne in 'The Problem of Evil' in Brown (ed.), *Reason and Religion*.

73 In addition to Phillips's many works, see, for example, David Wisdo, *The Life of Irony and the Ethics of Belief* (Albany: SUNY Press, 1993), especially pp. 92–101; Stephen Mulhall, *Faith and Reason* (London: Duckworth, 1994), pp. 18–19; and Ben Tilghman, *An Introduction to the Philosophy of Religion* (Oxford and Cambridge, MA: Blackwell, 1994), chapter 5. These are all formulations of what I take to be largely Wittgensteinian anti-theodicism.

74 This point about the 'obscenity' of theodicies is made particularly forcefully by Bernstein in his *Radical Evil*.

75 On the relation between the problem of evil and the distinction between genuine religiosity and pseudo-religiosity, see Sami Pihlström, 'Religion vs. Pseudo-Religion: An Elusive Boundary,' *International Journal for Philosophy of Religion* 62 (2007), 3–31. Cf. also Pihlström, *Pragmatic Pluralism and the Problem of God*, 'Conclusion'.

76 As noted above, this famous section in *The Brothers Karamazov* is also a major inspiration of Neiman's entanglement of the problems of evil and comprehensibility. I am not here making any claims about how Dostoevsky

DOI: 10.1057/9781137412669.0004

himself saw the matter; his novels, as is well known, are 'polyphonic' and full of tensions.

77   Marilyn McCord Adams, 'Ignorance, Instrumentality, Compensation, and the Problem of Evil,' *Sophia* 52 (2013), 7–26. Already in several previous writings, Adams has explored the possibility of responding to the problem of evil in specifically Christian terms (rather than purely metaphysical theism). See, for example, her paper, 'Horrendous Evils and the Goodness of God,' *Proceedings of the Aristotelian Society*, suppl. vol. 63 (1989), 297–310, reprinted in Eleonore Stump and Michael Murray (eds), *The Philosophy of Religion: The Big Questions* (Malden, MA and Oxford: Blackwell, 1999), pp. 250–7. Adams there argues that a Christian believer's intimate personal union with God may give her/his life profound significance even when that life is threatened by 'horrendous evils.' The critical questions to be posed below are relevant to the formulations of that earlier essay as well.

78   Adams, 'Ignorance, Instrumentality, Compensation, and the Problem of Evil,' p. 12 (original emphasis).

79   Adams, 'Ignorance, Instrumentality, Compensation, and the Problem of Evil,' p. 12.

80   Ibid., p. 13.

81   Ibid., p. 19.

82   Ibid., p. 20.

83   At this point, it should be noted that when I speak about 'victims' of evil and suffering, I fully recognize the problems troubling processes of victimization. The category of 'victim' can also be used for various purposes, good and evil. It can become an instrument in political power struggle. I am trying to use it as neutrally as possible here. It might be better to simply talk about 'witnesses' of evil, for instance – but then again, most potential witnesses do not survive to witness. See Giorgio Agamben, *Remnants of Auschwitz: The Witness and the Archive*, trans. Daniel Heller-Roazen (New York: Zone Books, 2002).

84   What I can offer here is only a very preliminary discussion of the concept. I will get back to the topic of recognition and acknowledgment in my metaphilosophical conclusion toward the end of the book.

85   Adams, 'Ignorance, Instrumentality, Compensation, and the Problem of Evil,' p. 21.

86   Ibid., p. 21.

87   Ibid., p. 22, n57.

88   Ibid., p. 22.

2

The Moral Luck, Reward, and Punishment of a Sick Soul

Abstract: *This chapter continues the anti-theodicist argumentation of the previous chapter by examining more deeply William James's pragmatist ethics and philosophy of religion, partly in comparison to some Wittgensteinian themes. It is argued that we should follow Wittgenstein in regarding moral reward and punishment as ultimately ethically irrelevant. It is then suggested that the Jamesian 'sick soul' views morality with a very special kind of seriousness. Evil and suffering cannot be eliminated or justified; there are no 'moral holidays' on offer. The chapter concludes with some comparative reflections on James and Paul Feyerabend.*

Keywords: James, W.; Wittgenstein, L.; Feyerabend, P.; sick soul; moral luck; theodicy; melancholy; tragedy; disharmony

Pihlström, Sami. *Taking Evil Seriously*. Basingstoke: Palgrave Macmillan, 2014. DOI: 10.1057/9781137412669.0005.

After the broadly Peircean characterization of evil as a 'real general' and the brief critique of theodicies in Chapter 1, this chapter will examine the relation between religion and morality from a Jamesian pragmatist point of view, focusing on the fundamental importance of a certain kind of *attitude* to the reality of evil and suffering. My discussion differs not only from mainstream philosophy of religion but also from many available treatments of pragmatist philosophy of religion and moral philosophy due to what I already above called the '*via negativa*' methodology. I am *not* trying to positively characterize, or to interpret James's characterizations of, such notions as the 'good life,' or the 'goods' or 'fruits' of religious life and religious experiences – even though I do regard Jamesian pragmatism as a highly valuable perspective on these concepts and topics as well. On the contrary, I want to examine the nature of ethically acceptable religious outlooks by drawing attention to evil, suffering, melancholy, and tragedy. In this sense, I will continue the ethical criticism of philosophy of religion – and philosophy generally – started in the previous chapter, although I will no longer directly cite contemporary theodicy theorists, for instance.

This chapter will, in any case, continue to develop the anti-theodicist approach to the problem of evil outlined in Chapter 1. This theme will now be approached from a possibly somewhat unusual angle in terms of the concepts of *moral luck, reward*, and *punishment*. A special attitude to these dimensions of morality is adopted, I will suggest, by the Jamesian 'sick soul' who is unable to take a 'moral holiday' from her/his engagement with evil and suffering and whose ethical attitude to life is therefore fundamentally melancholic.

My exploration of these issues will, I hope, offer a case study on how central issues in moral and religious thought can be illuminated 'through negation,' focusing on the *minimal* necessary conditions for the possibility of morality, instead of some 'maximal' dimensions of the good life at its best. Even though I will try to elaborate on this idea through a consideration of James's pragmatism, my discussion does not primarily aim at scholarly historical truth about what James actually said or thought. My discussion should, rather, be read as an attempt to philosophize 'with James' about these matters of vital importance. I have been struck by the way in which the piecemeal and pluralistic approach that James defends throughout his major works should not just be understood as a view emphasizing the plurality of positive – that is, happy, interesting, exciting meaning-bestowing, significant – experiences that human beings have

DOI: 10.1057/9781137412669.0005

in their (secular and/or religious) lives. Instead, the negative – that is, unhappy, absurd, threatening, melancholic, or tragic – experiences are at least as important as the positive ones.

Generally speaking, I agree with those who have emphasized the *tragic dimension of pragmatism* – the need to 'catch the deeper, darker tones of human articulation'[1] – in contrast to those who see pragmatism as a 'mere' philosophy of the good. (We might call the latter kind of pragmatists 'healthy-minded,' adopting James's terminology from a different context.)[2] Meliorism, to use another Jamesian term, in my view *presupposes* (instead of overcoming) a serious attitude to the reality of evil, the acknowledgment that we may not in the end be able to make the world a better place, even though we must always try.[3] There is, then, a tragic element inherent in pragmatic meliorism itself. While I am not entirely convinced that the notion of tragedy provides the best possible characterization of the Jamesian position regarding evil and suffering (see below), I do believe that James's concept of a *sick soul*,[4] and especially his account of the ethical and religious relevance of this concept, captures a great deal of what has been meant by the 'tragic sense of life.'[5]

The moral irrelevance of moral reward and punishment

Instead of beginning with direct comments on James's views, I want to start from issues in moral (and religious) education.[6] Philosophical issues of moral reward and punishment quite naturally arise in (early) moral education. When children are gradually initiated into moral thinking – for example, through traditional fairy tales – they usually learn that the good will eventually be rewarded and the bad 'will get what they deserve.' The protagonist in a fairy tale typically gets a reward after a morally heroic action, while the villains are punished or destroyed. Children thus relatively easily learn that morality is a system of rewards and punishments. This idea is also smoothly extended into moral reward and punishment conceived in religious terms. If the reward or punishment is not available 'in this world,' as it often isn't, then it is presumably to be understood as transcendent or supernatural: the good will be rewarded and the evil will be punished not here but in the hereafter; at some point the divinity will compensate for the injustices of this world – as we just saw Marilyn McCord Adams proposing (Chapter 1).

DOI: 10.1057/9781137412669.0005

The obvious problem here is that the child, when learning to adopt the moral perspective in terms of reward and punishment, may learn that one ought to act morally *in order to* eventually get the reward or to avoid the punishment. Admittedly, such a conception of morality may be a necessary intermediate stage in the process of one's moral maturation, but it can hardly be what we seriously ought to mean by the moral perspective or moral attitude. On the contrary, in contrast to an 'external' conception of morality as a matter of reward and punishment, we should presumably in moral education focus on an 'internal' conception, according to which the moral value of an action is based on the action itself. (We are here overlooking the differences between, say, deontological and utilitarian ethical systems – my concerns are more fundamental, or 'metaethical,' though on the other hand I am not committing myself to any standard division of labor between metaethics and normative ethics, either; see also Chapter 1.) The core of moral education should, arguably, be the attempt to lead the educated person (the child or the pupil) to see morality as something that inherently matters to us, not as a means to something else, such as a reward, but as something that, in order to function as morality at all, cannot be a means to *anything* external to itself. The motivating force of the moral perspective can arise only from within morality itself.[7]

James's 1891 essay, 'The Moral Philosopher and the Moral Life,' could be read in this light – not primarily as an examination of moral education but as a rejection of any theoretical foundation of morality that could be more fundamental than the moral perspective itself arising from our natural interests and needs as human beings.[8] Another key reference here is Wittgenstein, who remarks in the *Tractatus* that reward and punishment are irrelevant to ethics. Ethical value (or the lack of it) lies in the action itself – or, better, in one's entire life.[9] The ethical agent must not seek some future reward (or fear a future punishment) but must, rather, view her/his current action *sub specie aeternitatis* – as something that is itself a fundamental commitment to living a certain kind of life. The action cannot receive its moral value from its relation to anything external to itself.

This theme has been further developed in the Wittgensteinian tradition of moral philosophy by, among others, Peter Winch, who insightfully returns to the Socratic idea that 'nothing can harm the good man.'[10] After Aristotle's commonsensical acknowledgment that the good life encompasses several different elements and is thus also affected by

DOI: 10.1057/9781137412669.0005

highly contingent circumstances, this view may have seemed to many of us to be impossible to accept, although the Christian tradition has to some extent kept it alive – albeit at the cost of also keeping alive the confused conception of moral reward and punishment. Winch argues that morality is independent of mere worldly facts – anything agreeable or disagreeable – to the extent that nothing that contingently happens to a person can really hurt the one who acts morally. Insofar as that person has maintained her/his commitment to the moral perspective, that very commitment is more essential than anything disagreeable that might contingently take place in her/his life.

I am not referring to Wittgenstein and Winch in order to reflect any further on this peculiar Wittgensteinian tradition in ethics, or on its relation to pragmatism (which does deserve further elaboration).[11] I merely want to emphasize that these thinkers' criticism of the relevance of moral reward and punishment is something that the Jamesian pragmatist ought to take very seriously. What I am next going to say about moral luck, moral holidays, and the sick soul should be understood against this pragmatist-cum-Wittgensteinian background. In brief, the sick soul realizes that morality is not about reward and punishment and that no moral holidays are offered to us. This is a crucial application of the 'negative' methodology (outlined in the Introduction and Chapter 1) to the basic question of what morality means for us.

Moral luck and moral holidays

It is at this point that our discussion ought to be connected with the topic of *moral luck*, which has been debated by philosophers especially since Bernard Williams's and Thomas Nagel's seminal contributions in the 1970s.[12] The problem of moral luck is not just a marginal issue in moral philosophy; as Nagel has aptly remarked, it is ultimately a problem concerning the possibility of genuine moral agency: if the moral value of our actions is to a great extent a matter of luck, can we be regarded as truly responsible for anything?

The problem, in a nutshell, is that the shape one's life as a whole takes – and thus its moral value, or moral admirability or deplorability – may largely be a matter of luck: one cannot decide where and when one was born, for example, and such highly contingent external factors – in general, one's being at a certain place at a certain time – may crucially

DOI: 10.1057/9781137412669.0005

determine the course of one's moral actions (and omissions). One's being a good person and one's being, therefore, beyond life's contingencies in Winch's above-described sense ('nothing can harm the good man') are themselves, to a considerable degree, matters of contingent luck. One hardly deserves a reward or a punishment simply because one was, purely contingently, lucky or unlucky enough to be at a certain place at a certain time. Insofar as we are fortunate enough not to have lived in Nazi Germany, for instance, having to decide whether to risk our lives by saving Jews, we can deserve neither reward for our non-participation in the deportations nor punishment for our failure to assist persecuted families to escape. Yet, our relation to what happened to those who were unable to avoid such morally demanding circumstances (as well as our continuing reflections on that relation) may itself be an ineliminable feature of *our* moral agency and commitments today.

Now, it may be argued that taking seriously the idea that morality is not a matter of reward and punishment entails taking seriously the phenomenon of moral luck. On the other hand, there is a deep tension here. We are (and should be) reluctant to accept that matters that are most important for us – whether we are morally good or evil – could be a matter of sheer luck. Our goodness, if there ever is such a thing, is 'fragile,' as Martha Nussbaum has famously pointed out in *The Fragility of Goodness* (1986) and elsewhere.[13] Even so, mere luck *is* often rewarded: just think of lottery, for instance. Is moral life, or life in general, like this? We should, as a matter of acknowledging our precariousness and finitude generally, learn to think of life from the perspective of such radical contingency, and the concept of moral luck may be needed here.

We might conceptualize the 'reward' that cases of moral luck may provide us with in terms of James's concept of a *moral holiday*. We are lucky to have avoided (at least some) tragic moral choices, for instance. This 'lottery ticket' is rewarded to us as the possibility of taking a relatively relaxed and happy attitude to moral life. Just as we do not have to worry about our daily duties when enjoying a vacation, we need not worry about our not having helped the Jewish families that desperately tried to avoid deportation to concentration camps. As we haven't done anything we should feel guilty about regarding this historical event we were not part of, we can sit back and enjoy our moral holiday. Those who were less lucky – those who were there – are 'punished,' in a sense, by a bad conscience, or more severely by having had to make a tragic choice that haunts and will haunt them for the rest of their lives. Alternatively,

DOI: 10.1057/9781137412669.0005

we might say that we may be inclined to accept the 'fact' of moral luck without too much worrying about it, if we are (in James's terms) 'healthy-minded'; only the sick souls among us are truly and deeply concerned with this issue, and only for them is the reality of moral luck a phenomenon that makes their moral lives problematic from the start.

The concept of a moral holiday emerges in the context of James's criticism of the Absolute – that is, the postulation of Hegelian monistic idealists – and the related defense of pluralism. When he distinguishes between several different forms of monism (the idea of 'oneness'), the philosophically most controversial dimension of this idea is the notion of 'the one knower' – that is, the Absolute, a popular metaphysical postulate in the late nineteenth and early twentieth century among Hegelians, in particular. In this context, James argues that pragmatism prefers the pluralistic and empiricist approach to the monistic and rationalistic (or 'viciously intellectualistic') postulations celebrating the Absolute whose only pragmatic cash-value, according to him, is the occasional moral holiday it might grant us. The debate with monistic idealists' views, including particularly those of F.H. Bradley and Josiah Royce, was one of the most important controversies James engaged in, especially toward the end of his philosophical career. This is how he concludes the critical discussion of the problem of 'the one and the many' in *Pragmatism*:

> 'The world is one,' therefore, just so far as we experience it to be concatenated, one by as many definite conjunctions as appear. But then also *not* one by just as many definite *dis*junctions as we find. The oneness and the manyness of it thus obtain in respects which can be separately named. It is neither a universe pure and simple nor a multiverse pure and simple. And its various manners of being one suggest, for their accurate ascertainment, so many distinct programs of scientific work. Thus the pragmatic question 'What is the oneness known-as? What practical difference will it make?' saves us from all feverish excitement over it as a principle of sublimity and carries us forward into the stream of experience with a cool head.[14]

This, furthermore, is how James describes the 'moral holiday' in *Pragmatism*, again in relation to the Hegelian idealists' in his view ethically and metaphysically appalling postulation of the Absolute:

> What do believers in the Absolute mean by saying that their belief affords them comfort? They mean that since in the Absolute finite evil is 'overruled' already, we may, therefore, whenever we wish, treat the temporal as if it were potentially the eternal, be sure that we can trust its outcome, and, without sin, dismiss our fear and drop the worry of our finite responsibility. In short,

DOI: 10.1057/9781137412669.0005

they mean that we have a right ever and anon to take a moral holiday, to let the world wag in its own way, feeling that its issues are in better hands than ours and are none of our business.

The universe is a system of which the individual members may relax their anxieties occasionally, in which the don't-care mood is also right for men, and moral holidays in order, – that, if I mistake not, is part, at least, of what the Absolute is 'known-as,' that is the great difference in our particular experiences which his being true makes, for us, that is part of his cash-value when he is pragmatically interpreted. [...] If the Absolute means this, and means no more than this, who can possibly deny the truth of it? To deny it would be to insist that men should never relax, and that holidays are never in order.[15]

However, the fundamental Jamesian argument, ultimately, is *not* that we are entitled to take our moral holiday, either because of having been 'morally lucky' or for any other reason, but rather that there are in the end no moral holidays available. There is no possibility for any genuine rest or relaxation in moral matters. The rejection of the Absolute has this dramatic negative consequence. On the contrary, the Jamesian attitude to morality can be compared – as has been done by Megan Craig – to Emmanuel Levinas's demanding concept of moral agency and moral subjectivity, characterized by continuous 'vigilance' comparable to insomnia.[16] In short, we cannot sleep well if we attempt to take a moral holiday. Our moral luck of being able to relax on our vacation is immediately interrupted and destroyed by ethical insomnia: sooner or later we wake up to the bad conscience of having ignored human suffering and evil. Or if we don't – if we just continue to enjoy our holiday as if nothing ethically problematic ever happened around us – then we are hardly moral subjects in any serious sense at all. Then our holiday cannot be 'moral' but is, instead, *amoral*, comparable to the eternal 'holiday' that mere animals take from matters moral. We never have the moral luck of enjoying truly relaxing moral holidays insofar as we remain human beings.

As Craig emphasizes, just as the Levinasian self is characterized by constant ethical vigilance, James eventually rejects the moral holiday the Absolute could have guaranteed. We might say that the Jamesian pragmatist's moral holiday is thus (repeatedly, inevitably) interrupted by Levinasian 'insomnia' – the insomnia that 'turns into ethical wakefulness' and 'signifies both a risk and a hope: the risk of being subject to a day that never ends, and the hope of awakening to a world of faces that never close.'[17] James's 'strenuous mood' could, then, more or less

DOI: 10.1057/9781137412669.0005

be equated with Levinas's vigilance, and with the related conception of ethics as 'ongoing labor.'[18] The ethical project is endless and infinite: whatever we do, or fail to do, in our philosophical thought, or generally in our worldly actions, may have profound ethical significance. The Levinasian ideas that 'subjectivity *is* ethical subjectivity,' openness to the fragile other, and that 'ethics takes place in the dark,'[19] in the context of human suffering and vulnerability, are clearly Jamesian, too. Being a subject is to 'feel uncomfortable' most of the time, or rather always; in this sense, again, there are no moral holidays.[20] If ethics were captured in a single abstract principle, then we might enjoy occasional moral holidays, but no such luxury is available. Insomnia on a moral holiday is the human condition.

On the street with other people and (in one's insomnia) 'in the dark,' one must, then, be continuously aware of potentially ethically demanding situations, of others – or 'faces' – that one is responsible to and for.[21] Just as James remarked that we must not be 'deaf to the cries of the wounded,' Levinas, and Craig following him, emphasize 'the ethical importance of listening,' which means that a certain kind of 'passivity' is central in ethics.[22] This, however, is a very special kind of passivity, not opposed to moral action. Craig notes that there is 'passive activity in James' and 'active passivity in Levinas'; both view passivity as an ethical willingness, 'getting *past oneself* in order to wake up to a reality outpacing one's intentions.'[23] Levinas's breathtaking descriptions of fatigue and insomnia, carefully analyzed by Craig, are attempts to capture something from this special ethical mood. Vigilance, being awake, does not only entail acting intentionally but also remaining passively open to others. This passivity may itself be considered an aspect of 'negative thinking' explicated in Chapter 1.[24]

The 'happy man's' happy world and the 'sick soul's' guilty world

According to Wittgenstein's pre-Tractarian *Notebooks* (1914–16), the happy man and the unhappy man live in 'different worlds,' and the happy man's world is a 'happy world.'[25] These formulations can again be connected with the issue of moral luck. The happy person is lucky to live in the world s/he lives in. This is not something that s/he has chosen her/himself, or something s/he should be rewarded for, though. It is not an

DOI: 10.1057/9781137412669.0005

achievement of any kind. It is just the way the world is, for her/him, as a contingent result of (moral) luck.

What might be characterized as the deterioration or corruption of the seriousness of the moral perspective in contemporary societies may to some extent be a result of our failure to appreciate the depth of our contingency, including the central (yet extremely problematic) place that moral luck occupies in our lives. It is not easy for us to acknowledge that we *could* have been guilty of monstrous crimes just due to unlucky circumstances. If we live in a 'happy world', to echo Wittgenstein, or if we are 'healthy-minded' in James's sense, it may be extremely demanding for us to recognize *our own* human capacity for evil.

The notion of 'transcendental guilt'[26] might be brought to the picture right here. One reason to invoke such a concept is to highlight that we can never legitimately accept any moral self-satisfaction; or if we do, we are already taking a step out of the moral perspective. If we *are* morally good (should that ever be possible for us finite humans), we may be good simply because we are lucky. Hence, we do not deserve any moral reward – ever. There are no Nobel Prize discoveries in ethics, as Raimond Gaita perceptively remarks.[27] Nor do we necessarily deserve punishment, but we *might* at any time be or become guilty – and so we *are*, transcendentally, always already guilty in the sense that we can, and presumably should, view our entire lives under the aspect of guilt.

While guilt is seldom either Wittgenstein's or James's explicit topic, what Wittgenstein called the 'happy man' may be contrasted with what James called the 'sick soul' precisely regarding the way in which a sense of evil, guilt, and melancholy colors a sick soul's entire life. In *The Varieties of Religious Experience*, James tells us that the sick souls are those who, in contrast to the 'healthy-minded', maintain that 'the evil aspects of our life are of its very essence, and that the world's meaning most comes home to us when we lay them most to heart.'[28] The sick souls, then, are those 'who cannot so swiftly throw off the burden of the consciousness of evil, but are congenitally fated to suffer from its presence.'[29] Reflecting on the reality of evil and suffering, we may become 'melancholy metaphysicians',[30] acknowledging human helplessness and sadness even when life seems happy and easy. James concludes:

> The method of averting one's attention from evil, and living simply in the light of good is splendid as long as it will work. It will work with many persons [...]. But it breaks down impotently as soon as melancholy comes; and even though one be quite free from melancholy one's self, there is no doubt that

healthy-mindedness is inadequate as a philosophical doctrine, because the evil facts which it refuses positively to account for are a genuine portion of reality; and they may after all be the best key to life's significance, and possibly the only openers of our eyes to the deepest levels of truth.[31]

Therefore, James suggests, '[t]he completest religions would [...] seem to be those in which the pessimistic elements are best developed' – that is, 'religions of deliverance,' according to which one has to 'die to an unreal life' in order to be 'born into the real life.'[32]

The concept of a sick soul is, for James, a concept to be employed in the psychological and philosophical description and explanation of certain kind of religious attitudes and ways of living and thinking. However, given the close relation between religion and ethics in James, this concept can, I believe, be used in ethical contexts bracketing the actual religious aspects of, say, conversion. We may say that the sick soul takes seriously – ethically seriously – the evil and suffering around her/him in the world even if s/he never experiences this as a religious problem. The sick soul, then, acknowledges that (as James puts it toward the end of *Pragmatism*, without using this specific terminology) 'something permanently drastic and bitter' may always be in store for us, however successfully we fight against evil and suffering.

Insofar as we detach the notion of the sick soul from its immediate context in the psychology of religion, we may say that James writes in the same intellectual and spiritual setting in which Neiman and some other contemporary philosophical and political theorists of evil operate, a context in which evil is a challenge to our attempt to find life meaningful at all – a context *very* different from the theoretical context typical of mainstream evidentalist philosophers of religion.[33] Acknowledging evil and the potential disharmony[34] and even absurdity of life (individual and social), as well as the limits of philosophical theorization and reflection on these matters, while affirming an active, melioristic attitude (against an unavoidably tragic background), can be seen as a key Jamesian contribution to the problem of evil and to the challenge to reflect on the relation between religion and morality arising from this problem. According to James, as I read him, we should never philosophically theorize in a theodicist manner about the potential 'harmonious' justification, accommodation, or meaningfulness of evil and suffering. We should, rather, acknowledge evil and its victims by not attempting to explain it, or their sufferings, away; and we should simply fight against evil instead of accepting it by justifying it.

DOI: 10.1057/9781137412669.0005

In his posthumously published work, *Some Problems of Philosophy*, James contrasted pluralism and monism in terms of the problem of evil as follows:

> Evil, for pluralism, presents only the practical problem of how to get rid of it. For monism the puzzle is theoretical: How – if Perfection be the source, should there be Imperfection? If the world as known to the Absolute be perfect, why should it be known otherwise, in myriads of inferior finite editions also? The perfect edition surely was enough. How do the breakage and dispersion and ignorance get in?[35]

Accordingly, the theoretical approach of monists (for example, again, Hegelian idealists) leads to the theodicy problem, while the more practical approach of the pluralists (including James himself) starts from the acknowledgment that evil is real – not to be explained away or justified – and focuses on the task of 'how to get rid of it.' In *Pragmatism*, James argued against 'the airy and shallow optimism of current religious philosophy' that what suffering human beings experience '*is* Reality': 'But while Professors Royce and Bradley and a whole host of quileless thoroughfed thinkers are unveiling Reality and the Absolute and explaining away evil and pain, this is the condition of the only beings known to us anywhere in the universe, with a developed consciousness of what the universe is.'[36] A Leibnizian theodicy, in particular, postulating a 'harmony' of the universe, amounts to 'a cold literary exercise, whose cheerful substance even hell-fire does not warm'; hence, the idealist and optimist philosophers James argues against are, he says, 'dealing in shades, while those who live and feel know truth.'[37]

James's *Pragmatism* actually opens the entire project of advancing a melioristic philosophy with a discussion of the reality of evil – and in the final pages James returns to evil, suffering, loss, and tragedy:

> In particular *this* query has always come home to me: May not the claims of tender-mindedness go too far? May not the notion of a world already saved *in toto* anyhow, be too saccharine to stand? May not religious optimism be too idyllic? Must *all* be saved? Is *no* price to be paid in the work of salvation? Is the last word sweet? Is all 'yes, yes' in the universe? Doesn't the fact of 'no' stand at the very core of life? Doesn't the very 'seriousness' that we attribute to life mean that ineluctable noes and losses form a part of it, that there are genuine sacrifices somewhere, and that something permanently drastic and bitter always remains at the bottom of its cup?
>
> I cannot speak officially as a pragmatist here; all I can say is that my own pragmatism offers no objection to my taking sides with this more moralistic

DOI: 10.1057/9781137412669.0005

view, and giving up the claim of total reconciliation. [...] It is then perfectly possible to accept sincerely a drastic kind of a universe from which the element of 'seriousness' is not to be expelled. Whoso does so is, it seems to me, a genuine pragmatist.[38]

It is this very same moral seriousness that has been emphasized in the contemporary discourse on evil by Neiman, Bernstein, and others.[39] There is a sense in which our moral life with other human beings in a world full of suffering is inevitably tragic. This is because, given our human finitude, we will never be able to fully overcome evil and suffering; yet we must always, melioristically, try. Our moral seriousness is based on this realization of the tragic dimension of life. This is what the sick soul realizes, and this is what makes the sick soul's perspective on life superior to the 'healthy-minded' 'happy man's' perspective – even when the sick soul her-/himself is 'morally lucky' to enjoy relatively non-demanding ethical circumstances.

The concept of the sick soul has been discussed by commentators in great detail, but the ethical aspects of this notion still remain to be worked out. The sick soul, indeed, never enjoys a moral holiday in the way the Wittgensteinian happy man may do. Rather, the sick soul, suffering (as we may say) from an insomnia on a moral holiday, is fundamentally serious and melancholic. Her/his basic attitude to the world and life (which, again, if we follow Wittgenstein, 'are one') is the one of melancholy. Her/his *world* – not just her/his attitude to the world s/he lives in – is melancholic. This is not to say that it is necessarily an 'unhappy' world in the Wittgensteinian sense; rather, the very special ways in which a sick soul can be 'happy' must be understood against the background of such melancholy. Furthermore, this sophisticated moral attitude, instead of the naïve picture of moral rewards and punishments, should also be taken seriously in moral education. Even more importantly, it could even be argued that ultimately only the sick soul is, or can be, 'genuinely religious' (and perhaps genuinely ethical, too). A religious attitude, however enjoyable the positive fruits of religion may be, would then itself be inherently melancholic, affirming and reaffirming the seriousness of life.[40]

It may also be suggested that this kind of seriousness is part of James's very specific version of *realism*. By this we should not mean 'metaphysical realism.'[41] He was, in the pragmatic sense of the term, as fully a realist as anyone – especially when it comes to acknowledging the full reality, and the ethico-religious significance, of human suffering, mortality, and evil.

DOI: 10.1057/9781137412669.0005

It would be much more interesting to compare James's pragmatic realism to the 'realistic spirit' that Cora Diamond attributes to Wittgenstein,[42] at least if we purge Diamond's position from its anti-metaphysical and 'therapeuticist' aspects.[43] The ethical recognition of the full reality of evil and suffering is a crucial element of this realism, which, hence, is ultimately grounded in ethics, in the proper philosophical and experiential attitude we should take to other people around us, to the human voices we must hear. For the same reason, this form of realism is also pluralistic: there is no essence of evil and suffering but an irreducible individual variety – yet also generality – in them, very different voices, different 'cries of the wounded.'[44] Presumably Leo Tolstoy touches this polyphonic understanding of suffering as his narrator opens *Anna Karenina* by maintaining that all happy families are happy in the same way whereas unhappy families are each unhappy in their own specific ways. Yet, this does not prevent unhappiness, or evil, from being a Peircean-like 'general.'

Based on this plurality inherent in suffering, we may further suggest that James's realistic spirit, as applied to evil and suffering, is also a realism with *relational identities*. As James's radical empiricism, also called 'natural realism' by James himself, accepts the reality of relations in addition to the reality of particulars, we should make the even more radical observation that, from the perspective of Jamesian realistic spirit, there is no non-relational existence at all. In particular, our own personal identities are relational: we are what we are, the kind of experiencing subjects we take ourselves to be, only through our relations to other human beings in a common world with different human needs and interests always already in place. This position has obvious ethical and political significance.[45] This realism of the sick soul should, furthermore, be distinguished from, for example, metaphysical or scientific realism, which would presumably go better together with the 'healthy-minded,' in James's terminology (I will return to this point in due course).

Contingency, irrevocability, traces

Being a sick soul is, moreover, to be fundamentally – *melancholically* – conscious of and concerned with one's – and our generally human – mortality and finitude, as well as with the contingent traces one's actions (as well as omissions) leave in the world. Hence, the sick soul's ethical

DOI: 10.1057/9781137412669.0005

perspective emphasizes not only the reality but also the *irrevocability* of evil and suffering – an issue that has to some extent been emphasized in recent discussions of pragmatist moral philosophy and philosophy of religion.[46] Everything once real, including Auschwitz, is *forever* real. Our ultimate punishment (or, rarely, reward) in morality may be that whatever we do, or fail to do, leaves irrevocable traces into whatever futures, or future presents, we or our fellow human beings will inhabit.[47] Any human act (or omission) is radically contingent, excluding a myriad of possible worlds. Moral luck is a pervasive phenomenon, as we have seen, and its pervasiveness may make the demands of morality either illusory or, perhaps even worse, too tragic to live with. The sick soul melancholically reflects on the inevitability of this state of affairs, finding no peace in such reflection, thus once again recognizing the impossibility of ever taking a genuine moral holiday.

There is, then, a tension deeply involved in the sick soul's ethical (and/ or religious) engagement with the world. The sick soul recognizes, and acknowledges our need to continuously recognize, both *finitude* (human mortality and the resulting contingency) and a kind of *infinity* (irrevocability) – that is, our inability to ever heal all the wounds there are, to wipe suffering away. On the one hand, we always inevitably leave a trace in the world, whatever we do or fail to do; on the other hand, we will one day be gone and nothing will remain. Both the traces and the threatening nothingness pose us an existential challenge that may (possibly) be met only religiously, if at all.[48]

The notions of moral luck as well as reward and punishment should, further, lead us to appreciate the need of adopting a certain kind of *double perspective* on life and the world, a perspective analogous to Kant's distinction between the perspectives of nature and freedom, or science and ethics (or reason in its theoretical and practical use). There is a sense in which our lives, in their deep contingency, are necessarily out of our own hands, beyond our control; this is the perspective of moral luck (or, perhaps, the lack of such luck) – and, possibly, the perspective of an occasional moral holiday. But there is also the – transcendental, existential, metaphysical – perspective of radical freedom and responsibility: we are responsible for our personal interpretations of even the most contingent circumstances we occupy in a way we could never have chosen, that is, for matters of 'mere luck.' Hence our transcendental guilt and melancholy. This is comparable not only to the Jamesian sick soul's predicament but also to Jean-Paul Sartre's conception of 'freedom-in-a-situation': we may be just contingently, out of sheer luck, 'thrown into' a certain situation while retaining full responsibility for our interpretation of that situation, and of our situationality generally. This is our responsibility for how we manifest our humanity in the particular historical circumstances we find ourselves in. Any action we undertake, or avoid undertaking, leaves traces that will never be entirely wiped away. *Therefore* we need the 'via negativa' approach seeking to identify the *minimal* conditions of morality, not the maximum of good life. Very simply, we should leave as few evil traces in the world as possible.

To be able to live, or learn to live, with this double perspective is to be a mature human moral agent. More generally, Jamesian ethical investigations can be seen as reflections on (to put it in Kantian-like transcendental terms) the necessary presuppositions of our ability to make sense of ourselves as moral agents.[49] Recognizing our inability to eliminate or reduce away the tension between the two perspectives is to recognize a fundamental feature of our ethical finitude, of moral agency as we know it – something that James, arguably, recognized. It is not implausible to suggest that this recognition could itself be religious in an extended sense. Moreover, it is not implausible to suggest that it is a recognition that the Jamesian melancholic sick soul is capable of better than a healthy-minded and happy person. It is melancholy that drives James's project from the beginning to the end, all the way from the early essays from the 1870s and 1880s collected in *The Will to Believe* – including 'The Sentiment of Rationality,' 'Is Life Worth Living,' and others – up to, and including, the posthumous *Some Problems in Philosophy* (1911). It is melancholy that drives him to postulate a finite God that might help in our moral struggle, but also might not be able to guarantee a moral universe. Melancholy, in this sense, is compatible with a strenuous mood.[50]

'Real generals' again

This chapter has, I hope, made a case for the relevance of certain Jamesian concepts, especially the concept of a sick soul, in contemporary ethics and philosophy of religion by (re-)entangling them with some other ethical concepts (for example, moral luck) that have so far been discussed only from a quite different philosophical point of view. Accordingly, the

DOI: 10.1057/9781137412669.0005

issues I have examined are fundamentally important also outside James scholarship.

Our simple starting-point in this chapter – the moral education of the young through fairy tales in terms of the idea of moral reward and punishment – has led us to profound issues of moral luck, melancholy, tragedy, and guilt. These familiar concepts have by no means been exhausted in the philosophical elaborations they have so far received. There is further work to be done in reflecting on how exactly they shape our understanding of what morality means, or can mean, or should mean, for us. If there is one concept I would like to use to summarize all this, that concept must presumably be *finitude*. We are finite – mortal – in the sense of never being fully able to entirely take our lives into our own hands; our contingency and vulnerability, including the fragility of our moral goodness, are aspects of that finitude (and so is, therefore, our moral luck, or our lack thereof). Accordingly, the resources of the reward-and-punishment vocabulary are very limited, and therefore, the phenomenon of moral luck is much more central than is often admitted.

It might be suggested that it is our moral finitude itself that makes us (in Levinasian terms) moral insomniacs. The moral holiday is available only to those who illegitimately help themselves to the fairy-tale-like rhetoric of moral reward and punishment and who (equally illegitimately) feel able to sleep well as soon as the evil have been properly punished. Such a holiday is never offered to those who see moral reward and punishment (in the terms of Wittgenstein's *Tractatus*) 'in the action itself' and who simultaneously recognize (with James and his most perceptive pragmatist commentators) that any human action, however good or evil, leaves irrevocable traces in the world we live and act in. Human contingency is inextricably intertwined with this finitude. But our recognition of contingency and irrevocability may also give rise to the kind of melancholic reflection – the reflection the sick soul inevitably engages in – that enables us to see the profound, even religious, importance of morality. It is right here that, from a Jamesian perspective, morality and religion are ultimately inseparable. Both are deeply related to our often desperate attempts to understand and appreciate human life in a world full of evil, misery, and suffering; both are at their deepest when melancholic, primarily because of the infinity of the gap between what our lives are actually like and what they should become. The notion of the sick soul insightfully captures both the religious and the ethical aspects of this metaphysical melancholy.[51]

DOI: 10.1057/9781137412669.0005

At least one additional metaphysical issue remains to be considered here – if only in order to leave its further scrutiny for another occasion. As is well known, James's pragmatism emphasizes actual and concrete experience in comparison to Peirce's original version of the pragmatic maxim, which focuses on the *conceivable* – possibly never actualized – practical effects that the objects of our ideas might have. If Peirce's 'real generals' are real – if there are real *possibilia*, for instance[52] – then it could be argued that not only the actual facts and events of human history but also the mere possibilities that were never actualized are 'irrevocable' in the tragic sense described above. (This might, I suppose, be understood as a version of the Principle of Plenitude.) Then, not only actual horrors such as the Holocaust but all possible horrors would be irrevocably part of our ethical orientation to the world we live in and would need our moral attention. We should, reminded by what is actual, be aware of what is possible for us. We may look at such human possibilities with utter terror. As has often been remarked, the Holocaust showed us what human beings are capable of. So its horror is not merely in what actually happened, even though that is as horrible as anything can be, but also in what *could* happen. Sometimes the actual may simply shock us, as Peircean Secondness, in such a concrete way that we may be unable to even reflect further on any mere possibilities, but even amidst such shock effects there is room for the further realization that even something worse could have happened. We are always capable of more; even though we are finite and contingent beings, there is no upper limit to the suffering we can in principle inflict on other human beings. There is an *excess* in evil, as several commentators on the concentration camps, the paradigm of modern evil, have noted. Therefore there is also an excess in the extremity of humanly possible suffering, which in the camps led to a constant transgression of the boundary between the human and the non-human; as Agamben puts it, the 'almost infinite potentiality to suffer' is 'inhuman,' and accordingly 'humans bear within themselves the mark of the inhuman.'[53]

These troubling thoughts may be *both* rewarding, because we are also, melioristically, capable of making things better, *and* deeply troubling, because what we have arrived at here is – lacking a better word – a kind of (self-)punishment. We are not morally lucky enough to avoid the possibility of thinking seriously about what we could have done, or what we could and should have done otherwise, how we could and should have been better persons. Sometimes such mere possibilities – the wide

DOI: 10.1057/9781137412669.0005

gap between the ideal and the actual – may lead us to irrevocable moral horror and possibly require religious surrender.[54] Yet, again, Jamesian pragmatism may offer us resources to live with – *not* to avoid but to live with – such horror.

Abundance and disharmony

There is a further dimension to be added to the discussion of pragmatist (both Peircean and Jamesian) versions of *realism* – that is, a certain kind of *'abundance' or 'richness' (or variety) of existence*, including both nature and the human cultural world.[55] It is right here that I want to introduce another point of comparison that may be helpful in appreciating some of James's insights, namely, Paul Feyerabend. This comparison could yield a form of pragmatism standing firmly against any 'foundation' of ethics (or of science, for that matter), taking seriously the plurality of human 'voices' we need to hear in our world-engagements. Thus, it may add a crucial further dimension to my attempt to provide a pragmatist approach to the 'negativities' our lives depend on. What the James-Feyerabend comparison may teach us is that we should not attempt to construct either our ethical or scientific thought on a 'positive' foundation; rather, we should, as has been argued throughout this chapter and the previous one, begin from negativities such as evil, suffering, and finitude, and let the human voices that express them be heard. Both James and Feyerabend argue that we should let a wide variety of practice-embedded perspectives open, in our individual and social attempts to know, and to cope with, the world we inhabit. Culturally and politically, this position is opposed to what both thinkers found an intellectually and ethically narrow-minded scientism; we can also see these two philosophers as defending a deeply *democratic* view of experience against scientific 'imperialism.' Richness here means *diversity* and *irreducibility*, which can be understood as ethical and aesthetic but also metaphysical ideas (or, perhaps better, ideals). However, this does not presuppose the doctrine Feyerabend is notorious for, that is, the 'epistemologically anarchist' thesis that 'anything goes' – not, at least, in its received and often ridiculed formulations. One can develop a pragmatist appreciation of the abundance of irreducibly different perspectives in a much more plausible and responsible way.[56]

DOI: 10.1057/9781137412669.0005

It must be noted that Feyerabend's radical views (like James's in their own way) are often radical primarily, or at least partly, because of his wild rhetorical style. Some of his apparently anti-scientific statements do go too far by any reasonable lights, but it is, I think, obvious that he held no clearly anti-scientific views for that matter. What he is opposed to is a certain philosophical understanding of science, and a certain philosophical picture of science as part of culture. In his campaign against dogmatic and, as we may say, 'imperialist' views of science, he clearly joins James, although he rarely, if ever, directly refers to James (nor has his philosophy of science been usually discussed in the context of pragmatism scholarship – with the possible exception of Rorty's neopragmatism). Feyerabend's points of contact with James – or, better, philosophical views that can be developed by synthesizing some of their key ideas – include at least the following overlapping proposals, which I here offer not as detailed accounts of his (or James's) thought but as openings hopefully leading to intensified discussions of these matters.

First, both thinkers subscribe to theoretical and methodological *pluralism* (but not radical relativism or anarchism – keeping in mind that it is not easy to clearly keep these allegedly different positions apart): there should be a plurality of rival theories, scientific as well as ethical, to be tested not only against reality but against each other. Secondly, they insist on 'saving' human beings and their natural social and cultural practices from the 'tyranny of science' and the 'dehumanizing' effects of Western science – and from any totalizing and therefore dehumanizing ideology. This idea(l) incorporates both metaphysical and ethical dimensions, emphasizing the need to critically examine the scientific worldview and its historical development from a broader ethical and cultural perspective. This entails an anti-reductionist celebration of abundance, the richness of the world, and the *disunity* of science, in contrast to any reductionist picture of unity and harmony (metaphysical, ethical, or aesthetic).

A natural corollary of this is, thirdly, the need to save *particularity* by avoiding exaggerated generalizations (that is, what James called 'vicious intellectualism'): individual perspectives and experiences are crucial for our world-categorization and -engagement, both ethically and metaphysically (and even aesthetically as well as religiously or theologically). Thus, fourthly, for Feyerabend as much as for James, truth – scientific truth, in particular – is ultimately grounded in *ethics*: an ethical attitude to both the richness of the natural world and the history of human

DOI: 10.1057/9781137412669.0005

traditions and culture is a starting point for any serious inquiry. Finally, this entails taking *disharmony* seriously: these philosophers are against theodicies of all kinds (religious, non-religious, secular, scientific), as we have already clearly seen in James's case. The world-order is not neat and harmonious; there is real evil, misery, and suffering; furthermore, there is also genuine 'otherness' not reducible to a single totality. We may thus come to appreciate the Jamesian arguments against theodicies *via* a quite different philosophical route, by appreciating Feyerabend's unique contribution to the philosophy of science.

For these positions celebrating abundance, disharmony, and anti-theodicy – insofar as they can be articulated as philosophical positions – we may find textual evidence in Feyerabend's posthumously published writings, in particular.[57] In *Conquest of Abundance* (1999), Feyerabend begins by rejecting any 'grand dichotomy' between 'a solid, trustworthy, genuine reality on one side and deceiving appearances on the other.'[58] Dichotomies between the real and the apparent, between knowledge and mere opinion, and (in religious traditions) between righteousness and sin have been introduced throughout our history in order to 'conquer abundance'; in this historical process, 'views that reduce abundance and devalue human existence' have become very powerful, and Feyerabend wants to explain why.[59] Scientific realism, in particular, has ideologically and dogmatically sought to reduce away the variety of ontologies, the richness of what is 'real.'[60] James would have been pleased to agree with Feyerabend that '[s]cience certainly is not the only source of reliable ontological information,' and he would have been equally pleased to join Feyerabend in attacking the mistake of identifying some particular 'manifest reality' developed within science with 'Ultimate Reality'[61] – which, in Kantian terms, would be equivalent to the mistake of identifying the empirical world with things as they are in themselves.

We cannot deal with the details of Feyerabend's complicated historical narrative, beginning from the Greeks,[62] but we should note striking analogies to the kind of picture that James arrives at through his pragmatist critique of problematic dualisms and dichotomies. Just like James (and, arguably, Wittgenstein), Feyerabend connects philosophical and scientific argumentation intimately with human life-practices: 'Arguments about reality have an "existential" component: *we regard those things as real which play an important role in the kind of life we prefer.*'[63] Arguments, that is, have power only insofar as they conform to 'nonargumentative pressures,' and it is partly for this reason that there cannot be any 'clear

DOI: 10.1057/9781137412669.0005

and lasting line between the "objective" and the allegedly "subjective" ingredients in the process of knowledge acquisition and of knowledge itself.'[64] This position can easily be compared to James's account of 'philosophical temperaments.'[65] In viewing the history of philosophy as a history of clashes of philosophical temperaments, James also appreciated both 'subjective' and 'objective' dimensions in our knowledge-seeking and argumentation. Our objective epistemic projects are inevitably rooted in our subjective attempts to make sense of our existence, and there is no principled dichotomy to be drawn between these aspects of our ethical, aesthetic, and epistemic lives. We can see Feyerabend's work as offering a recent variation on this Jamesian theme.

An 'ontological (epistemological) pluralism,' Feyerabend further argues, is 'closer to the facts and to human nature' than any 'unitarian realism' about 'Ultimate Reality.'[66] Science itself is inherently pluralistic and full of conflicts;[67] Feyerabend argued already in his famous papers in the 1960s that scientific progress 'comes through "*theoretical pluralism*", allowing a plurality of incompatible theories, each of which will contribute by competition to maintaining and enhancing testability, and thus the empirical content, of others.'[68] As an example of Feyerabend's later defense of the richness of scientific and non-scientific perspectives on the world – arguably employing a version of the 'pragmatic method' – consider the following:

> Now if science is indeed a collection of different approaches, some successful, others wildly speculative, then there is no reason why I should disregard what happens outside of it. Many traditions and cultures, some of them wildly 'unscientific' [...] succeed in the sense that they enable their members to live a moderately rich and fulfilling life. Using this extended criterion of success I conclude that non-scientific notions, too, receive a response from Nature, that Nature is more complex than a belief in the uniformity and unique excellence of science would suggest [...].[69]

Furthermore, just like James in a *constructivist* vein suggested that real things are those that serve our interests and needs in pragmatically efficacious ways, and are hence 'made' more than just found by us, Feyerabend argues that scientists are 'sculptors of reality,' not merely acting causally upon the world but also '*creat[ing] semantic conditions* engendering strong inferences from known effects to novel projections and, conversely, from the projections to testable effects.'[70] Our 'entire universe,' he tells us in his characteristically exaggerating tone, 'from the mythical Big Bang via the emergence of hydrogen and helium, galaxies, fixed stars, planetary

DOI: 10.1057/9781137412669.0005

systems, viruses, bacteria, fleas, dogs to the Glorious Arrival of Western Man is an *artifact*.'[71]

The metaphoric reference to 'sculptors' should be taken seriously. Feyerabend not only rejects standard dichotomies between the subjective and the objective or between the real and the apparent; he also questions the absoluteness of the lines we draw between art, science, and nature. In his 1994 essay, 'Art as a Product of Nature as a Work of Art',[72] he suggests that 'works of art are a product of nature, no less than rocks and flowers,' while conversely 'nature itself is an artefact, constructed by scientists and artisans, throughout centuries, from a partly yielding, partly resisting material of unknown properties.'[73] Our 'intellectual generalizations' around notions such as art, nature, and science are to be pragmatically understood as 'simplifying devices that can help us order the abundance that surrounds us,' as 'opportunistic tools, not final statements on the objective reality of the world.'[74] Again, James would clearly have agreed. Insofar as 'we inquirers construct the world in the course of our inquiries' – as Preston summarizes Feyerabend's late view[75] – presumably Dewey could have agreed as well, given his view that the objects of inquiry are constructed through, or arise from, inquiry instead of existing 'ready-made' prior to inquiry.[76]

I am not claiming that Feyerabend's (or James's) view, which clearly is intended as ethically and politically relevant, is easy to accept. On the contrary, the challenge common to all forms of *pragmatic realism* as a middle path between radical relativism and metaphysical realism haunts every attempt to say that 'Nature is not something formless that can be turned into any shape; it resists and by its resistance reveals its properties and laws,'[77] while maintaining the 'sculptor' metaphor. So, the world (or Nature) has 'its' ('its own'?) properties and laws, after all? As Preston observes, Feyerabend occasionally endorses views that no one would deny but that are not relativist while occasionally subscribing to genuine relativism but failing to show why it ought to be accepted.[78] The pragmatists' (including James's) troubles with maintaining a compromise between realism and relativism have a similar structure. In any event, I think it is fair to say that Feyerabend, just like the pragmatists – both classical pragmatists like James and contemporary neopragmatists like Hilary Putnam – seeks a middle path between metaphysical realism and relativism, arguing that the world can be categorized in a plurality of different ways serving different human interests, while admitting that the world in some sense (which is hard to articulate clearly) 'resists' our

DOI: 10.1057/9781137412669.0005

attempts to describe it. As sculptors of reality, we cannot just sculpt our world into any shape we just happen to prefer.

This pursuit of a middle path is directly relevant to the main concern of this chapter and the entire book, namely, the need to deal with the reality of evil. This is above all because both James and Feyerabend insist on the fundamental role played by ethics in relation to both ontology and science. In my *Pragmatist Metaphysics* (2009), I examined James's use of the pragmatic method as a method of tracing out the pragmatic core of metaphysical disputes (concerning, for example, substance, the free will, theism, or monism vs. pluralism) in terms of their ethical dimensions.[79] Unfortunately I overlooked the fact that Feyerabend had already in his 1992 paper, 'Ethics as a Measure of Scientific Truth,'[80] observed that 'ethics (in the general sense of a discipline that guides our choices between forms of life) affects ontology.'[81] This is exactly the point that James makes and that a true pragmatist, in my view, should make, because 'real' is, for us pragmatists, *'what plays an important role in the kind of life one wants to live.'*[82] The reference to our 'wanting' to live a certain kind of life may be problematic here, though. We may not want to live a life in which the paradigmatically 'real' thing is a pile of corpses resulting from a mass murder, but this is precisely the kind of reality we cannot, given our more general human needs and interests, ignore. Our ontological acceptance of such a reality – a 'realistic spirit' regarding evil – is ethically commanded.

We should, Feyerabend proposes, argue not from allegedly objective scientific facts to norms (for example, human rights) but the other way around 'from the "subjective", "irrational", idiosyncratic kind of life we are in sympathy with, to what is to be regarded as real.'[83] This is again slightly toward the extreme, but it does recapitulate James's point about the ethico-metaphysical significance of philosophical temperaments – or, to put this in a more Wittgensteinian terminology, the dependence of ontological commitments on forms of life. Moreover, it highlights the way in which our need to respond to evil and suffering – and any other moral challenges we face – 'sculpts' our very existence. Hence the ethical *and* ontological significance of the kind of issues discussed here. Moreover, insofar as ethics guides our 'sculpting' efforts, it is this 'realistic spirit,' instead of a metaphysically realistic account of reality, that should be preserved in our ethical reflections on how to most appropriately categorize the world.

Turning, finally, to those of Feyerabend's late ideas that are available in the 2011 volume, *The Tyranny of Science*, based on a set of lectures delivered

DOI: 10.1057/9781137412669.0005

in 1992, it is again interesting to observe that when Feyerabend considers the relation (and potential conflict) between the great discoveries of modern science and the negative features of modernity – 'war, murder, cruelty' – he is in a way asking the same questions that James struggled with in his attempt to philosophically accommodate both the scientific worldview and the human need to make ethical (and aesthetic) sense of the world. The philosopher's task is an *emancipatory* one: human beings need to be freed from the 'tyranny of science,' that is, the tyranny of the dogmatic picture according to which there is just a single way things objectively are. In particular, the idea of a 'harmonious world' – whether scientifically or theologically elaborated – cannot be an ethically sound postulation.[84] Similarly, as we have seen, James asked why there should be any eternal harmony and worried that postulating such a harmony commits a theodicist fallacy (as we may call it).

Now, Feyerabend perceptively shows that science can take the role of a theodicy. What he opposes – and what James opposes as well – is the dichotomous picture of reality according to which there is a 'perfect but inhuman order' (either scientific or theological) over and above the 'stupidity and disorder' of human life and reality.[85] And what he is concerned with, just like James, is the scientistic and materialist view that the scientific world-picture offers us a 'world without purpose,' a 'frozen universe of solitude.'[86] Such a conception of science can, however, be democratically criticized, because scientists themselves are not the final authority on 'the use of their products,' including the interpretation of science itself.[87] In short, '[q]uestions of reality are too important to be left to scientists.'[88] Now, instead of unity, what we truly experience is diversity and difference; and if, as good empiricists (and again like James), 'we take experience as our only guide,' then 'we must say that there is diversity, not unity.'[89] Feyerabend, then, offers an updated version of the 'piecemeal pluralism' James subscribed to in *A Pluralistic Universe* (1909). He also returns to the worry that the advancement of science may have 'de-anthropomorphized' and 'de-humanized' nature, 'until humans themselves were no longer viewed in a humane way,' and argues strongly against the idea of 'value-free' science, insisting that 'values play an important role in the constitution of scientific facts.'[90] James, once again, would happily agree.

One way of cashing out the issues concerning eternal harmony versus conflict that both thinkers were preoccupied with is, as Feyerabend explains, in terms of the choice between Sophocles and Plato. Whereas

DOI: 10.1057/9781137412669.0005

Plato wanted 'tragedy to be replaced by a view of good and bad which permits an escape from the bad and which doesn't have [a] tragic conflict in it,' Sophoclean tragedies find the world 'inherently contradictory' and thereby see it as containing a 'tragic dimension.'[91] Feyerabend, in a Jamesian manner, admits that it is largely a matter of individual philosophical temperament how we should judge this matter. As to whether to follow Plato or Sophocles, he says, 'it's up to whoever considers the question.'[92] As human beings, we face the fundamental issue of living with our philosophical views individually. For individuals like James and Feyerabend, Sophocles is clearly the winner of this dispute. The tragic sense of life, articulated in a Sophoclean way, may also accommodate the worries about traces and irrevocability reflected on earlier in this chapter.

We will return to some Feyerabendian reflections – especially on the intimate relation between the human being and her/his philosophy – in the final, more metaphilosophical chapter (Chapter 4). At this point, however, another comparative perspective on Jamesian pragmatism needs to be introduced.

Notes

1   Vincent Colapietro, 'The Tragic Roots of Jamesian Pragmatism,' forthcoming in *Journal of Speculative Philosophy* (2014), ms., p. 19. (I warmly thank Professor Colapietro for sharing a draft of this paper with me.)
2   James, *The Varieties of Religious Experience*, Lectures IV and V.
3   James develops meliorism especially in Lecture VIII of *Pragmatism*. This is a view lying between optimism, according to which a positive outcome (or the salvation of the universe) is guaranteed, and pessimism, according to which our situation is ultimately hopeless.
4   This concept is explored by James in *Varieties*, Lectures VI and VII. See further below.
5   We should duly note that the phrase, 'pragmatism and the tragic sense of life,' was coined by Sidney Hook in his book with the same title: see Hook, *Pragmatism and the Tragic Sense of Life* (New York: Basic Books, 1974). However, I am not going to deal with Hook's (largely Deweyan rather than Jamesian) version of pragmatism in any detail here. For Hook, tragedy is not so much a matter of dealing with evil as it is of dealing with the conflicts of goods with other goods. It should also be noted that the phrase, 'the tragic sense of life,' originates with Miguel de Unamuno, who was influenced by James. See de Unamuno, *Tragic Sense of Life*, trans. J.E. Crawford Flitch

DOI: 10.1057/9781137412669.0005

(New York: Dover, 1954; originally in Spanish, 1913), available online at Project Gutenberg: http://archive.org/stream/tragicsenseoflif14636gut/14636.txt. James is, clearly, a thinker with a philosophical temperament very close to this famous Spanish writer. Another European philosopher James might be fruitfully compared in this context is Gabriel Marcel: very much like Marcel's existentialism and Christianity, Jamesian pragmatism can be seen as a response to a 'broken world.' (Cf. Michael Rodnick's paper on Marcel's relation to American Philosophy at the 39th Meeting of the Society for the Advancement of American Philosophy, New York, March 2012.)

6   A case can also be made for the relevance of James's pragmatism to education, although James (unlike Dewey) was never a major philosopher of education. In particular, the 'will to believe' strategy, requiring a leap to an unforeseeable future and a recognition of human possibilities without sufficient evidence, plays a key role in such an attempt to reconstruct a Jamesian philosophy of education. See Sami Pihlström and Ari Sutinen, 'William James's Educational Will to Believe,' in Pauli Siljander, Ari Kivelä, and Ari Sutinen (eds), *Theories of Bildung and Growth: Connections and Controversies between Continental Educational Thinking and American Pragmatism* (Rotterdam: Sense Publishers, 2012).

7   I have dealt with this theme more comprehensively in some of my Finnish writings, including my essay, 'Satujen moraaliopetukset: Mietteitä moraalikasvatuksesta, ansiosta ja armosta' [The Moral Lessons of Fairy Tales: Thoughts on Moral Education, Merit, and Mercy], *Kasvatus* 36 (2005), 89–100. However, this discussion hasn't so far been adequately incorporated in my main works on (pragmatist) moral philosophy; cf. Pihlström, *Pragmatic Moral Realism: A Transcendental Defense* (Amsterdam: Rodopi, 2005a), and *Transcendental Guilt*.

8   This essay is available in James, *The Will to Believe*. As a reading of James's moral philosophy based on this essay, I recommend Sergio Franzese, *The Ethics of Energy: William James's Moral Philosophy in Focus* (Frankfurt: Ontos, 2008); cf. also Sarin Marchetti's forthcoming book, *The Moral Philosopher: Ethics and Philosophical Critique in William James*. For further discussion, see Pihlström, *Pragmatic Pluralism and the Problem of God*, chapter 4.

9   See Wittgenstein, *Tractatus*, § 6.422. Moreover, 'world and life are one' (Wittgenstein, *Tractatus*, § 5.621) – cf., for example, Stokhof, *World and Life as One* – as discussed both above in Chapter 1 and in my *Transcendental Guilt*, chapter 5.

10 See Peter Winch, *Ethics and Action* (London: Routledge and Kegan Paul, 1972); and Winch, *Trying to Make Sense* (Oxford and New York: Blackwell, 1987).

11 See Pihlström, *Pragmatic Moral Realism*, for comparisons between pragmatism and Wittgensteinianism.

DOI: 10.1057/9781137412669.0005

12 See Thomas Nagel, 'Moral Luck', in his *Mortal Questions* (Cambridge: Cambridge University Press, 1979); Bernard Williams, *Moral Luck* (Cambridge: Cambridge University Press, 1981). One aim of this chapter is to connect these usually disconnected debates; moral luck is only very seldom discussed in relation to moral reward and punishment. For an excellent overview of the central literature on the problem of moral luck, see Dana K. Nelkin's entry 'Moral Luck', in *Stanford Encyclopedia of Philosophy* (available online, 2008).

13 Martha Nussbaum, *The Fragility of Goodness* (Cambridge, MA and London: Harvard University Press, 1986). On the idea that life is fundamentally tragic because we are always unable to do everything we ought to do, to relieve or even notice all the suffering we ought to, and so forth, see also Nussbaum, *Love's Knowledge* (Oxford: Oxford University Press, 1990), especially the chapter on Henry James's *The Golden Bowl*. Nora Hämäläinen, in her insightful review of my *Transcendental Guilt* in *Journal of Value Inquiry* 45 (2011), 373–8, wonders what my 'transcendental argument' about guilt adds to Nussbaum's acknowledgment of this tragic dimension of life (or to, for example, Iris Murdoch's metaphysics of goodness); she may very well be right that it doesn't add much. (This is not the proper place to continue discussions of 'transcendental guilt' at length, though.)

14 James, *Pragmatism*, p. 73.

15 Ibid., Lecture II. Note that James's criticism of Kant and transcendental philosophy generally does not lead to any approval of Hegel's views (as in the case of some other pragmatists, including, for example, Joseph Margolis, who might find pragmatism a critical historical development of Hegel's critique of Kant). On the contrary, the Hegelian idealists (for example, Bradley and Royce) are from the Jamesian point of view simply unable to respond to the problem of evil in any ethically adequate manner. However, James's reaction to Schopenhauer – instead of Kant and Hegel – might be more interesting to study (and has not been much studied). This is another critical response to Kant, yet hostile to any theodicies along Hegelian lines and thus including a full recognition of evil. It might be in Schopenhauer's more existential (if not existentialist) orientation that nevertheless begins from a certain form of transcendental idealism that James's most interesting connections with the Kantian transcendental tradition emerge. However, again, there are significant differences: as a meliorist, James could never fully subscribe to Schopenhauer's pessimism.

16 Megan Craig, *Levinas and James* (Bloomington: Indiana University Press, 2010). See also my review of this volume in *Transactions of the Charles S. Peirce Society* 48 (2012), 108–11. (I'm here adopting some formulations from that review.) See also Critchley's remark on insomnia as an experience of a

DOI: 10.1057/9781137412669.0005

'fundamental openness of the human being to something that will not let it rest' (*How to Stop Living and Start Worrying*, pp. 42–3).

17   Craig, *Levinas and James*, pp. 15, 30.

18   Ibid., p. 93.

19   Ibid., p. 4.

20   Ibid., p. 109.

21   Craig may here de-emphasize Levinas's (and James's) religious aspects more than is necessary. I am not quite convinced that her description of Levinas's faith as 'a-religious' is correct – this strikes me as too strong, as it surely would in James's case – but there is certainly a true core to the idea of secularizing divinity in terms of the face of the other person (Craig, *Levinas and James*, pp. 92–3). If there is something like faith available to the Levinasian-Jamesian ethical subject, this must, we are told, be a faith where 'the only afterlife is the life of another person who lives on after one's death, and where a holy place is a crowded street' (Craig, *Levinas and James*, p. 93). However, this clearly wouldn't have been enough for James, who was interested (while avoiding dogmatic belief) in the possibility of survival and immortality in a more literal sense.

22   Craig, *Levinas and James*, p. 55.

23   Ibid., p. 84.

24   If Levinas's moral philosophy is a natural point of comparison for Jamesian pragmatism, another recent 'postmodern' option for such comparisons, more explicitly within the philosophy of religion, is offered by Richard Kearney's *anatheism*. Kearney proposes a return to God and faith 'after the death of God,' especially after the death of the God of theodicies. See Richard Kearney, *Anatheism: Returning to God after God* (Bloomington: Indiana University Press, 2012). The sick soul, we might say, *is* an 'anatheist' rather than being (or being able to be) a theist in the conventional sense (especially insofar as theism is related to theodicism). A more comprehensive discussion of the very interesting relations between pragmatism and anatheism must, however, be postponed to another occasion.

25   Ludwig Wittgenstein, *Notebooks 1914–1916*, ed. Elizabeth Anscombe and G.H. von Wright (Oxford: Basil Blackwell, 1961), note on July 29, 1916. Similar remarks occur in a condensed form in the *Tractatus* (§ 6.43).

26   See Pihlström, *Transcendental Guilt*.

27   Gaita's penetrating analyses of the moral perspective, particularly the ways in which that perspective and its seriousness are constituted by a certain kind of understanding of something's being a possible object of *remorse*, are available in his two major works, *Good and Evil: An Absolute Conception*, rev. edn (London and New York: Routledge, 2004; 1st edn 1991) and *A Common Humanity* (London and New York: Routledge, 2000). The remark about

DOI: 10.1057/9781137412669.0005

Nobel Prizes is in *Good and Evil*, p. 281. My *Transcendental Guilt* is crucially indebted to, though not always in agreement with, these reflections by Gaita.

28   James, *Varieties*, p. 114.

29   Ibid., p. 116.

30   Ibid., p. 121.

31   Ibid., pp. 137–8.

32   Ibid., p. 139.

33   See Chapter 1. On this difference between Jamesian pragmatism (interpreted in an anti-theodicist manner) and theodicist philosophy of religion, see also my *Pragmatic Pluralism and the Problem of God*, chapter 5.

34   The notion of disharmony will be revisited toward the end of this chapter in relation to Paul Feyerabend's views, which can be regarded as equally anti-theodicist as James's.

35   William James, *Some Problems of Philosophy: A Beginning of an Introduction to Philosophy* (1911), in *The Works of William James* (1977), p. 138. See also James, *Varieties*, p. 115. For a more recent – and more political – defense of pluralism against totalitarian monisms reducing human behavior to a 'single principle', see Tzvetan Todorov, *The Totalitarian Experience*, trans. Teresa Lavender Fagan (London: Seagull Books, 2011), especially p. 63.

36   James, *Pragmatism*, pp. 20–1.

37   Ibid., pp. 20, 22. Some of these remarks were already cited in the context of the theodicy vs. anti-theodicy discussion of chapter 1.

38   James, *Pragmatism*, pp. 141–2.

39   For references see Chapter 1.

40   In addition to, say, Levinas and Kearney, James's reflections might at this point be compared to yet another 'postmodern' thinker, Critchley, already briefly discussed in Chapter 1. See his book, *How to Stop Living and Start Worrying*, for reflections on lack, melancholy, and original sin highly relevant to my concerns in this chapter.

41   See my criticism of Michael Slater's metaphysically realistic reading of James in Pihlström, 'Realism and Pluralism in Pragmatist Philosophy of Religion'.

42   See Diamond, *The Realistic Spirit*. Putnam also finds this conception of realism important (though not uncontroversial) both as a reading of Wittgenstein and as a general philosophical approach. Cf., for example, his essays on Wittgenstein in Putnam, *Philosophy in an Age of Science*.

43   For a critical comment on too strongly (dogmatically) therapeutic readings of Wittgenstein and the pragmatists, see Sami Pihlström, 'A New Look at Wittgenstein and Pragmatism', *European Journal of Pragmatism and American Philosophy*, 4:2, www.journalofpragmatism.eu (2012).

44   As one of the few recent theorists of evil inspired by pragmatism, Richard Bernstein, explains (without specifically referring to these Jamesian considerations), there is no essence of evil; rather, evil can take very different

DOI: 10.1057/9781137412669.0005

forms in different and ever changing historical situations. See, again, Bernstein, *Radical Evil* and *The Abuse of Evil*.

45   On the importance of James's conception of relational identities, see José Medina, 'James on Truth and Solidarity: The Epistemology of Diversity and the Politics of Specificity,' in John J. Stuhr (ed.), *100 Years of Pragmatism: William James's Revolutionary Philosophy* (Bloomington: Indiana University Press, 2010), pp. 124–43.

46   Cf. here Claudio Viale's excellent paper, 'Royce and Bernstein on Evil,' *Contemporary Pragmatism* 10 (2013), 73–90; as well as Colapietro's above-cited essay, 'The Tragic Roots of Jamesian Pragmatism,' where Colapietro returns to Hook's conception of the tragic sense of life by noting that 'the losses most properly felt as tragic are significant and irrevocable, thus sorrowful and unredeemable' (ms., p. 2). Viale's discussion should make us rethink the conventional conception of Josiah Royce (as a pragmatist postulating the Absolute) as a thinker seeking to offer us a theodicy, even though theodicism in my view does seem to threaten the ethical acceptability of Royce's position, too. Royce's reflections on irrevocability and sorrow are highly relevant to the Jamesian concerns of this essay, even though I must almost entirely neglect Royce's position here. We may, I think, still see Royce as offering a theodicy, although a sophisticated one, invoking the notion of the suffering God. Cf. Josiah Royce, 'The Problem of Job' and 'The Religious Mission of Sorrow,' both available in vol. 2 of *The Basic Writings of Josiah Royce*, ed. John J. McDermott (New York: Fordham University Press, 2005). (Cf. also another recent essay by Claudio Viale: 'William James' Conception of Religion in Josiah Royce's Mature Thought: Three Approaches' [forthcoming, available at Academia.edu], which Dr. Viale kindly shared with me. I should note that while I am largely sympathetic to Viale's careful explorations of James and Royce, the kind of secularized and ethical characterization of the sick soul that I have offered – going beyond James's own views to some extent – is in a mild tension with Viale's claim that there is no '*moral* salvation' available for the sick souls: 'morality never cures' [ms., pp. 9–10]. This is undoubtedly true if we focus on what James actually says about the possibility of salvation the sick soul faces, but if we take into account not just the *Varieties* but also *Pragmatism* and other late works, we will be forced to admit that the philosophical view of religion available to the Jamesian pragmatist is itself thoroughly ethical, to the extent that any religious metaphysics that is humanly possible must have ethical grounds, even if religion itself – or the notion of salvation in particular – cannot be reduced to ethics. Life in general is a moral struggle for the Jamesian pragmatist; viewing religion and morality as parts of the same overall project of finding, or constructing, meaning is not to maintain any specific conception of salvation – a topic I am glad to leave for theologians to discuss further.)

DOI: 10.1057/9781137412669.0005

47   I am indebted to Hans Joas's comments on this idea.

48   While this chapter, or book, does not explicitly address James's views on death and mortality (for my earlier discussions of that topic, see Sami Pihlström, 'William James on Death, Mortality, and Immortality,' *Transactions of the Charles S. Peirce Society* 38 [2002], reprinted in an expanded form in Pihlström, *'The Trail of the Human Serpent Is over Everything,'* chapter 3), it seems to me clear that human mortality – or, more generally, vulnerability and potential helplessness – is a key source of the sick soul's attitude to the world: 'The fact that we *can* die, that we *can* be ill at all, is what perplexes us, the fact that we now for a moment live and are well is irrelevant to that perplexity. We need a life not correlated with death, a health not liable to illness, a kind of good that will not perish, a good in fact that flies beyond the Goods of nature' (James, *Varieties*, p. 121).

49   I am grateful to Marcus Willaschek for a conversation that led to this formulation.

50   Cf. further reflections on this in comparison to Hans Jonas's in the next chapter.

51   In a more comprehensive discussion of the relations between ethics, religion, and metaphysics in James, it would have to be examined how, for instance, he deals with the 'human contribution' in shaping the world into what it is for us. This idea itself has an interesting evolution, from the 'M+x' idea of 'The Sentiment of Rationality' (1879, available in *The Will to Believe*) to the somewhat more sophisticated ethics-metaphysics entanglement of the third and fourth lectures of *Pragmatism* (1907) and the ontological constructivism defended in the seventh lecture of that book. The unifying thread of this development is the idea that practical – moral, emotional, agency-related – considerations do not just play an additional role shaping our attitudes to what the world is like but contribute to our basic understanding of the world itself, and, insofar as 'we' and the world cannot be completely separated, to the way(s) the world is. Our ethical perspective partly defines what a metaphysical problem or question for us *is*. How we find the world to be – or the problems we find ourselves to be forced to examine – is dependent on the plurality of practice-laden perspectives from which the world opens itself to us.

52   See Chapter 1 for a brief account of evil as a real general. For a discussion of Peircean real generals in relation to both Peircean and Jamesian versions of pragmatism, see Pihlström, *Pragmatist Metaphysics*, chapter 6.

53   Agamben, *Remnants of Auschwitz*, p. 77 (see also p. 133).

54   It would be a further intriguing task to connect this discussion with Deweyan philosophy of religion, particularly with the Deweyan conception of God as an active union of the ideal and the actual. See John Dewey, *A Common Faith* (New Haven, CT: Yale University Press, 1991; first published

DOI: 10.1057/9781137412669.0005

1934); cf. also Pihlström, *Pragmatic Pluralism and the Problem of God*, chapter 2. The notion of surrender (or, possibly, its Deweyan analogue, cosmic piety) might also be relevant here in the sense that the sick soul may, when exhausted by experiences of evil and guilt, finally surrender to a wider reality believed to be actual – for example, in a Christian context, to God. In a sense, then, the self itself would be reduced to nothingness. This 'de-selfing' or 'un-selfing,' thematized by mystics like Simone Weil among many other thinkers, would again be an instance of negative thinking. However, there is a kind of dialectics at work here: self-surrender seems to presuppose a self that surrenders and is in a sense an active decision by the self. In self-surrender, one paradoxically still actively engages with oneself. The challenge for pragmatism is to find a way of moving beyond this simple dichotomy of activity and passivity – but that is a matter that needs to be discussed in more detail elsewhere.

55   This is a theme that could also be connected with Hannah Arendt's views on natality, to be commented on in the next chapter in relation to Hans Jonas's post-Holocaust ethics. The topic of abundance is relevant to what has been discussed in the Jamesian context in this chapter because it also points toward a recognition of the value of new perspectives, new beginnings, genuine novelty – which seem to unite Jamesian pragmatism and the defense of human individuality and particularity against 'absolutist' and totalitarian ideas and practices.

56   In order to set the record straight, we should briefly consider the notorious 'anarchist' thesis. Feyerabend is usually portrayed as a radical epistemological relativist and anarchist, according to whom 'anything goes.' There is no such thing as *the* scientific method; instead, science, according to Feyerabend, cannot be normatively distinguished from other human practices and discourses, in principle even from fairy tales and other clearly non- or pseudo-scientific discourses or practices. See the general presentations of Feyerabend's views in Eric Oberheim, 'Feyerabend, Paul K. (1924–94),' in John R. Shook (ed.), *Dictionary of Modern American Philosophers* (Bristol: Thoemmes Press, 2005); and John Preston, 'Paul Feyerabend,' in *Stanford Encyclopedia of Philosophy*, available online: http://plato.stanford.edu/entries/feyerabend/ (2009); cf., for example, Ilkka Niiniluoto's fierce criticism of Feyerabend in Niiniluoto, *Is Science Progressive?* (Dordrecht: Reidel, 1984), and Niiniluoto, *Critical Scientific Realism* (Oxford and New York: Oxford University Press, 1999). Thus, Feyerabend has even come to play the role of someone who is an *enemy* of science and reason – a paradigm case of irresponsibly relativist thinking. His reputation was not particularly helped by his infamous defense of creationists in the 1980s. By extension, this anarchism, when moved to the ethical and political realm, would allow any imaginable violations of fundamental moral principles and human rights, including

DOI: 10.1057/9781137412669.0005

Nazism. For this reason, it has been important for pragmatists, as well as many other serious thinkers committed to normatively governed inquiry (in science and ethics), to carefully distinguish their views from Feyerabend's. For example, philosophers sympathetic to James have often insisted that Jamesian pragmatism, despite its pluralism and anti-reductionism, is *not* a Feyerabendian-styled 'anything-goes' doctrine, even though it may occasionally have been mischaracterized as such. It is, thus, not a species of relativism or subjectivism. Indeed, already during his life-time – before Feyerabend was even born – James had to face misinterpretations (due to G.E. Moore and Bertrand Russell, in particular) picturing him as a radical relativist or subjectivist. In fact, in my own survey of pragmatist philosophy of science and its history a few years ago, I maintained the following: 'The pragmatist does not hold, with Paul Feyerabend [...], that "anything goes", or that a pluralist proliferation of scientific practices and methods is a good thing as it stands, because scientific practices have their own in-built normativity, and normative distinctions between good and bad science are internal to those practices themselves, hence something that the pragmatist ought to take seriously. However, this does not mean that the norms of scientific methodology would be handed down to us from above; to the contrary, science is a continuing critical process, in which not only theories but the methods used to justify them are constantly open for reevaluation. Instead of celebrating pluralism and anarchy as such, the pragmatist follows Dewey in emphasizing the *critical* function of philosophy, its role as "the critical method for developing methods of criticism" [...]'. (Sami Pihlström, 'How (Not) to Write the History of Pragmatist Philosophy of Science,' *Perspectives on Science* 16 [2008], 26–69, here p. 43.) On the other hand, in the same essay (p. 52), I also posed the following question: 'If, as I suggest, we approach [Thomas] Kuhn as a pragmatist (or pragmatic realist), should we also acknowledge Feyerabend [...] – the anarchist and arch-relativist – as a pragmatist, in some sense?' My answer was positive, at least 'inasmuch as we also acknowledge [Richard] Rorty's entitlement to the word "pragmatism".' This is because, while Feyerabend avoids committing himself to the pragmatist (or any other) tradition, he does speak about 'pragmatic philosophy' when referring to people or groups 'participating in the interaction of traditions'; such pragmatic philosophy is required for the 'open exchange' between people and traditions that is, in turn, needed to transcend simple relativism. (Cf. Paul Feyerabend, *Against Method: An Outline of an Anarchistic Theory of Method* [London: Verso, 1975; 3rd edn, 1993], pp. 217–18, 226–8.) Therefore, I concluded that Feyerabend's pluralism, anti-essentialism, and anti-foundationalism are clearly close to pragmatism, especially James's pragmatism. This is the line of thought I here want to continue in more detail. Even if we have – as we do – good reasons, including pragmatic reasons, to

DOI: 10.1057/9781137412669.0005

oppose the unacceptably relativist consequences of the 'anything goes' thesis, we may find valuable insights in Feyerabend's position, insights that may be employed by the kind of Jamesian ethical thinker whose profile I have sketched earlier in this chapter.

57 See Paul Feyerabend, *Conquest of Abundance: A Tale of Abstraction versus the Richness of Being*, ed. Bert Terpstra (Chicago and London: The University of Chicago Press, 1999), and Feyerabend, *The Tyranny of Science*, ed. Eric Oberheim (Cambridge: Polity Press, 2011; first published in Italian in 1996). I will in the following refer to these sources rather than to the classical work, *Against Method*.

58 Feyerabend, *Conquest of Abundance*, p. 9.

59 Ibid., pp. 13, 16.

60 Ibid., p. 122.

61 Ibid., pp. 145, 214.

62 In this sense, Feyerabend's narrative is comparable to Dewey's versions of historical criticisms of misleading dichotomies that also typically begin from antiquity. See, for example, John Dewey, *The Quest for Certainty: A Study on the Relation between Knowledge and Action* (1929) (Boston: G.P. Putnam's Sons, 1960).

63 Feyerabend, *Conquest of Abundance*, p. 71 (original emphasis).

64 Feyerabend, *Conquest of Abundance*, pp. 78–9.

65 James, *Pragmatism*, chapter 1.

66 Feyerabend, *Conquest of Abundance*, p. 215.

67 See Ibid., p. 239.

68 Preston, 'Paul Feyerabend', §2.10.

69 Feyerabend, *Conquest of Abundance*, p. 195.

70 Ibid., p. 144.

71 Ibid., p. 224; cf. p. 240.

72 Feyerabend, *Conquest of Abundance*, chapter 8.

73 Ibid., p. 223.

74 Ibid.

75 Preston, 'Paul Feyerabend', §2.16.

76 This is a theme Dewey develops in his major work, *The Quest for Certainty*. See also, for example, Pihlström, 'How (Not) to Write the History of Pragmatist Philosophy of Science'.

77 Feyerabend, *Conquest of Abundance*, p. 238.

78 Preston, 'Paul Feyerabend', §2.15.

79 See Pihlström, *Pragmatist Metaphysics*, especially chapters 3–5.

80 This is also available in Feyerabend, *The Conquest of Abundance*, chapter 9.

81 Feyerabend, *The Conquest of Abundance*, p. 247.

82 Ibid., p. 248 (original emphasis).

83 Ibid., p. 251.

DOI: 10.1057/9781137412669.0005

84   Feyerabend, *The Tyranny of Science*, p. 11.
85   Ibid., p. 25.
86   Ibid., p. 35.
87   Ibid., pp. 35–6, 51.
88   Ibid., p. 51.
89   Ibid., p. 38.
90   Ibid., pp. 94–5.
91   Ibid., pp. 61–2.
92   Ibid., p. 62.

DOI: 10.1057/9781137412669.0005

3

A Suffering God and Post-Holocaust Pragmatism

Abstract: *This chapter continues the 'anti-theodicist' articulation and development of Jamesian pragmatism by introducing some previously unnoticed comparisons between Jamesian pragmatism and Hans Jonas's approach to ethics and metaphysics, which largely emerges from the need to deal with the Holocaust. For example, James's and Jonas's accounts of the 'finite God' are examined against this background. Their conceptions of the relation between ethics and metaphysics are strikingly similar but also point toward important differences.*

Keywords: James, W.; Jonas, H.; Holocaust; ethics; metaphysics; God; finitude; theodicy; anti-theodicy

Pihlström, Sami. *Taking Evil Seriously*. Basingstoke: Palgrave Macmillan, 2014. DOI: 10.1057/9781137412669.0006.

Scholars of William James, some of whom I cited in the previous chapter, have for a long time duly recognized that James's pragmatism does not simply amount to a naively forward-looking advocacy of instrumental reason, let alone a theory of truth according to which the truth of beliefs is simply reducible to their utility. It is also widely understood that James starts his philosophical reflections on truth, rationality, religion, and related topics from an acknowledgment of the undeniable reality of evil, suffering, and mortality. It has been noted, for example, that *Pragmatism* both begins and ends with a discussion of death.[1] Our need to deal with, and live with, our mortality is thus the (or at least *a*) context within which James's philosophical project receives one of its most mature articulations. It has, furthermore, been argued (as I have also just done) that James's philosophy of religion offers no theodicy – that is, no solution to the problem of evil that would justify the theistic belief in the face of the empirical reality of evil and suffering – but seeks to come to terms with the full, shocking reality of evil that inevitably and irresolvably haunts religious believers' desires to arrive at neat metaphysical systems postulating an eternal divine harmony. True, James is a philosopher of life, celebrating individual human beings' capabilities of making a difference in the world, and even a philosopher seeking to articulate a theory of the possibility of life after death,[2] but as we saw in the previous chapter, he is at least as much a philosopher of melancholy, tragedy, and human finitude for whom no philosophical theory of, or 'solution' to, the serious problems of life can ever be more than tentative and provisional.

James, of course, was a pre-Holocaust thinker whose treatment of evil could never have achieved the pregnancy of some post-Holocaust philosophers' painful reflections on the moral catastrophes of the twentieth century. Even so, we may learn a lot from critical comparisons between James's pragmatism and views emerging from quite different philosophical traditions in the twentieth century.[3] A highly illuminating perspective on James's thought is provided, for instance, by the recent comparison to Levinas's ethics offered by Megan Craig.[4] For the purposes of this chapter, I have chosen to examine another 'Continental' thinker in close – and up to now mostly overlooked – relation to James: Hans Jonas. I believe that this comparison proves particularly useful when we try to reflect on the topics of evil, suffering, tragedy, and death in a Jamesian spirit. Jonas's philosophy has only very seldom, if ever, been read along with James's. One of the very few scholars who can be said to be deeply engaged with both thinkers is Richard Bernstein, a leading

DOI: 10.1057/9781137412669.0006

contemporary figure situated on the borderlines of pragmatism, critical theory, and 'Continental' philosophy more generally.[5] Even Bernstein, however, does not seem to find very much common ground between Jamesian pragmatism and Jonas's work on ethics and philosophy of religion.

In the following, I will present my critical comparison of James and Jonas as a brief catalogue of what I regard as their fundamental agreements and one perhaps equally fundamental disagreement (which, however, can be softened, as I will propose). As James has already been discussed at some length in the previous chapters, I will here allow more space to my citations of Jonas. My main source will be Jonas's posthumously published collection of essays, *Mortality and Morality: A Search for the Good after Auschwitz*,[6] containing some of his most important writings on the need to rethink both ethics and religion after the Holocaust. A comprehensive treatment of Jonas's thought employing all his major publications cannot be my task in a single chapter; it would require an entire book. This chapter should therefore be considered only a first step toward an appreciation of some of the striking analogues between Jonas's and James's ethical and religious thought. Paying due attention to those analogues may, I hope, be helpful in our attempt to take evil seriously, to develop a richer philosophical perspective on our need to respond to the presence of evil in the world we live in.

Naturalism, transaction, and relationality

Let us start from Jonas's most obvious agreement not only with James but with the pragmatist tradition generally: naturalism. Both Jonas and the pragmatists defend non-reductive and non-scientistic forms of naturalism, according to which both metaphysics and ethics need to be grounded in our natural existence as human beings. The pragmatists were presumably the first philosophers to emphasize Charles Darwin's lesson to philosophy. Whatever moral or metaphysical ideas we entertain, they must, in order to be taken seriously today, be compatible with what we know about the evolution of the human life-form. (This, of course, is not at all to claim that morality would be reducible to any scientific facts about the evolution of moral behavior.)

More specifically, life in its natural form is for Jonas a good-in-itself. In particular, future human life matters. There is a certain kind

DOI: 10.1057/9781137412669.0006

of purposiveness inherent in natural existence as such. Human freedom and self-transcendence emerge from our fully natural, embodied existence and its organic needs.[7] As the editor of *Mortality and Morality*, Lawrence Vogel, explains, according to Jonas we have a duty to humankind as such; the idea of humanity is part of the idea of purposive nature. This yields a duty to children in particular, which is why Jonas finds an archetype of responsibility in the parent's care for the child, perpetuating the capacity for responsibility itself.[8] Thus, the key principle of Jonas's naturalistic ethics is that we must 'safeguard and nourish the presence of human responsibility on Earth.'[9]

Jonas's naturalistic metaphysics, however, is by no means reductionistic or scientistic. It is even compatible with a 'cosmic piety' toward 'the whole of which we are a part.'[10] This can be regarded as a 'Deweyan' theme in his thought; among the pragmatists, it was Dewey (rather than James) who insisted on the idea of 'natural piety.'[11] Jonasian naturalism is, in any event, a natural starting point for an ecological ethics that in a pragmatic manner looks to the future – to the preservation of future human generations and their new ways of articulating human responsibility – instead of looking back to aprioristic principles or unchangeable moral codes. Our ethical theorization needs to be adjusted to the specific natural circumstances we live in, circumstances that may now be seriously threatened due to the current ecological crisis.[12] And pragmatists, clearly, have always maintained that we should start our reflections and inquiries, ethical as well as scientific, from the concrete practical circumstances we are in, seeking to creatively transform those circumstances, turning what Dewey called 'problematic situations' to non-problematic ones.

However, naturalism as such, though non-reductive, is not enough for a comprehensive philosophical approach. What is needed is a philosophical theory of what is natural for us as human beings in particular. Therefore, both James (and pragmatists generally) and Jonas can be seen as engaging in a philosophical study of 'human nature,' or *philosophical anthropology* (though usually without using that label). Jonas offers us three key examples of things distinctively human: the tool, the image, and the grave.[13]

The first of these is, obviously, a topic familiar both from pragmatism (especially Dewey) and Heidegger.[14] The image, in turn, especially in its 'biological uselessness,'[15] leads us farther beyond the animal than the tool does, because animal artifacts directly satisfy vital needs but this need not be the case with human images. However, the grave is the most

DOI: 10.1057/9781137412669.0006

distinctively human artifact, signifying the exclusively human recognition of mortality. While the tool embodies human freedom and the image signifies the human concern for the possible (in addition to the actual), the grave signals the emergence of reflection and, most importantly, self-reflection, expanding 'from the individual ego to the whole of existence.' Hence, 'metaphysics arises from graves.'[16]

All three artifacts considered by Jonas are 'modes of mediacy and freedom': the tool leads to technology and physics, the image to art, and the grave to metaphysics. The grave, moreover, 'tells us that a being, subject to mortality, reflects about life and death, defies appearances, and raises his thinking to the realm of the invisible, utilizing tool and image for this purpose.'[17] Hence, without the grave even the tool and the image would have a much more restricted use than they actually have in human forms of life.

The third point of comparison I want to invoke is more Deweyan than Jamesian. Whereas pragmatists, especially Dewey, have emphasized human beings' continuous interaction – or, better, *transaction*[18] – with their natural environment, seeking to conceptualize inquiry and knowledge-acquisition in such dynamic terms, Jonas perhaps somewhat surprisingly speaks about *metabolism* as an important philosophical concept. We constantly need to use, reuse, and process elements of the world we live in simply in order to survive. As Douglas Davies, a major scholar of death-related practices, has put it in another context, 'we sit in the world and eat it.'[19] We then process what we have eaten into – well, some more world. And we take in more of the world in order to continue this processing. Again, this is part of our natural existence which should not remain unfamiliar to our philosophy.

Metabolism, for Jonas, even serves as the defining characteristic of life. All life is *Stoffwechsel*, exchange of matter with the environment. Yet the living being in some sense remains the same through the processes of transaction in which its constitutive matter in the course of time completely changes. Here 'we are faced with the ontological fact of an identity totally different from inert physical identity, yet grounded in transactions among items of that simple identity.'[20] This is not in the end very far from James's relational conception of personal identity. We are, and constantly become, the individuals we are through our relations to the world around us; we are not atomistic, self-contained individuals whose ontological identity would remain untouched no matter happened outside us.[21]

DOI: 10.1057/9781137412669.0006

Metabolism is ultimately related to death. Eating the world, we kill. And eventually we will ourselves perish through the processes of transaction that now keep us alive. Hence, this central naturalistic concept that opens us to the perspective of naturalistic ethics needs to be returned to when we move onto consider the grounding of morality in mortality (see below).

Anti-theodicy and divine finitude

Moving into a more seriously ethical terrain, we should note that both James and Jonas are equally fundamentally anti-theodicist thinkers. That is, they refuse to respond to the problem of evil by offering anything like a theodicy, either religious or secular. This is also one of the aspects of Jonas's philosophy thoroughly discussed by Bernstein.[22] Not only are theodicies that are taken to justify or legitimize evil and suffering within, say, God's overall supremely benevolent plan usually theoretically unconvincing and implausible; much more importantly, they are, especially in our world after Auschwitz, immoral or even obscene. No decent ethical thinker can claim – after the atrocities of the twentieth century – that *all this* serves some hidden divine purpose. There is, as already argued in Chapters 1–2, no morally acceptable way in which we could explain away the brute reality of evil.

This is a key starting point not only for James, who argues that even 'hell-fire cannot warm' the cold exercises of Leibnizian or Hegelian theodicies,[23] but also for Jonas, who states the following:

> And when in horror we look at the pictures from Buchenwald, at the wasted bodies and distorted faces, at the utter defilement of humanity in the flesh, we reject the consolation that this is appearance and the truth is something else: we face the terrible truth that the appearance is the reality, and that there is nothing more real than what here appears.[24]

There is nothing more real than what here appears. Nothing, for us post-Holocaust human beings, can be more real – nothing can be more real in the ethically demanding sense of our being unable to fail to focus our attention to it – than the ultimate suffering of the victims. Had James lived to witness the twentieth century, he would undoubtedly have subscribed to Jonas's statement.[25]

Note that reality, according to Jamesian pragmatism, is in a special sense dependent on our selective attention.[26] We 'construct' what is real

DOI: 10.1057/9781137412669.0006

for us through our interest-driven, purposive habits of action; it is a general pragmatist idea that our ontologies always serve some human interest or have a practical function. Now, the 'wasted bodies and distorted faces' of the camps of the twentieth century, while certainly not serving any ordinary interest we might have, command us to focus our attention in a very special way, not to forget their reality. The demand they set us is moral. They could be seen as *ethically real* in a sense primary to any (merely) metaphysically construed reality.[27]

It must, furthermore, be observed that James's and Jonas's religious differences inevitably make their responses to the theodicy problem somewhat different. Jonas has repeatedly emphasized that there is a sense in which the problem of evil – especially in its post-Holocaust version – is even more difficult for the Jew than it is for the Christian. This is because from the Jewish point of view, God is 'the lord of history,' and this is particularly difficult to explain 'after Auschwitz.'[28] Moreover, the Jews who died in the Holocaust died *not* because of their faith or for the sake of their faith – martyrdom had been rendered impossible in their utter dehumanization – but simply anonymously and inhumanly, deprived of any reason to die.[29] When Jonas finds it necessary to rethink both the nature of ethical duty and the concept of God after Auschwitz, he engages in this rethinking within the Jewish tradition, while James, of course, offers us his version of rethinking from the perspective of liberalized Christianity – albeit without any dogmatic creed. Even so, both end up with strikingly similar pictures of the divinity.

Jonas's and James's common doctrine of a finite, limited God follows directly from their anti-theodicist reactions to the reality of evil. How could a benevolent God have allowed anything like the Holocaust to take place? The Holocaust, epitomizing all past and future genocides, is not only a tormenting challenge to philosophy and ethics but also to religion. Famously, it led people like Theodor Adorno to question the very possibility of poetry 'after Auschwitz'; it should lead us all to reconsider, if not question, the possibility of rational thinking in general. It is particularly important to reconsider ways of thinking about God, insofar as we feel the need to think in terms of this concept at all.

Just like James refused to postulate an infinite God – the kind of Absolute his major philosophical opponents, the British and American Hegelian monistic, absolute idealists like Bradley and Royce postulated[30] – Jonas also, when seeking to renew the concept of God 'after Auschwitz,' thematized the idea of a processual, finite, and suffering God.

DOI: 10.1057/9781137412669.0006

James once suggested that God himself may 'draw vital strength and increase of very being' out of our having faith in him.[31] That is, God is not supremely powerful and absolute but actually needs believers' faith in order to continue existing and fighting for the salvation of the universe. Jonas similarly suggests that 'His welfare depends on our fulfilling the promise of goodness that His gift of life offers us.'[32] God is limited, or better, 'self-limiting' and 'self-contracting.'[33] As Vogel puts it, according to Jonas, 'the only deity worthy of our devotion, given the magnitude of evil in the world, is a caring, suffering, and becoming God who is helpless to prevent evil.'[34] This God, for either Jonas or James, is neither the traditional absolutely sovereign God of theodicy nor the skeptical theist's 'hidden God' (*deus absconditus*) whose hidden purposes we cannot possibly disclose. Jonas's God – the only God he finds us able to have faith in after Auschwitz – is a God of 'contraction, withdrawal, self-limitation,' a God who 'renounced his being, divesting himself of his deity' in order to allow human life, and thus inevitably death, to emerge.[35] Jonas's God is, hence, a suffering and becoming God, but also a caring God 'involved' with the world and human beings.[36] In a rather Jamesian tone of voice, Jonas even speaks about 'an endangered God, a God who runs a risk.'[37]

The crucial observation here is that such a God cannot be omnipotent; in fact Jonas finds the very notion of 'absolute power' self-contradictory. Omnipotence would lead precisely to the utterly un-Jewish notion of a hidden, completely unintelligible God whose reasons for allowing evil would be entirely incomprehensible to us – or else to the equally problematic view that God is not good.[38] For related reasons, though of course not for any Jewish reasons, James also rejects the omnipotence of God. We human beings, living amidst evil and suffering, could – to put in Jamesian terms – have no 'intimate relation' to such an abstract and unintelligible deity; we could not 'feel at home' in a universe ruled by such a divinity.

This is not to say there would be no differences in James's and Jonas's conceptions of God and religious faith. Jonas is sympathetic – though not overly sympathetic – to Bultmannian 'demythologizing' approach to religion,[39] while James famously investigated mystical states of consciousness and was at least tempted to embrace – though perhaps never fully embraced – a form of supernaturalism. These differences, however, are relatively minor in comparison to the general ethical thrust of their philosophies of religion.[40]

DOI: 10.1057/9781137412669.0006

Ethics and metaphysics, theology and philosophy

Indeed, both Jonas and the pragmatists, especially James, find ethics and metaphysics (and religion) inextricably entangled, inseparably inter-twined. When reflecting on our ethical duty, we need to have a correct metaphysical picture of what our existence is like; conversely, that very picture already contains ethical elements and has ethical implications (as was seen above). The ethical rules and principles derived from Jonas's naturalistic premises are pragmatic and melioristic – and in this sense close to James's.

The ethical goals we pursue should, moreover, be modest enough, aiming at realistic improvements to the human situation.[41] In this way, Jonas, like James, stands firmly opposed to *both* nihilism or pessimism, according to which there is nothing to be done because everything is doomed to failure in the end, *and* utopianism or optimism, according to which nothing really needs to be done because the good will ulti-mately inevitably prevail.[42] The need to steer a middle course between those equally implausible extremes follows from our human nature. The ethics pragmatically needed must be compatible with a non-reductively naturalistic metaphysics and philosophical anthropology; there can be no pure ethics independently of such considerations about our nature as human beings, and our specifically human needs, interests, and capacities.

Just like ethics and metaphysics are entangled, theological and meta-physical ideas are also inseparable. In particular, the doctrine of a finite God is deeply rooted in a process-metaphysical understanding of reality in general and divine reality in particular. The suffering God is also a God always in the state of becoming.

It is crucial to observe that neither Jonas nor James believes that theol-ogy, or religion, could be the foundation of philosophy or ethics. Jonas famously regards theology as a 'luxury of reason.'[43] Moreover, he sees religious faith as a possible answer to such spiritual longings that are not strictly speaking 'needs of reason' in the Kantian sense. These 'longings' are, first, the need to react to the metaphysical question 'How did it all begin?' by invoking a personal 'loving presence,' and secondly, more existentially, to sustain the idea that nothing good is permanently lost or forgotten: 'that there be an eternal memory even of those innocent chil-dren whose lives have been cut short throughout history by "pestilence, war, and famine"'.[44] However, these 'longings,' instead of being regarded

DOI: 10.1057/9781137412669.0006

as mere 'luxuries', could be seen as 'needs' of the Jamesian 'whole man in us', the total human being not reducible to reason but incorporating emotion and will, that is, the 'passional nature' that is inevitably at work in our *weltanschaulichen* commitments that cannot be decided purely rationally.[45] Or, alternatively, they could be seen as 'needs' of the human being that Wittgenstein speaks about when remarking that when an individual human being feels her-/himself to be lost (*verloren*), this is the greatest possible torment, *die höchste Not*, which can be greater than the torment of the entire world.[46]

One of the deepest philosophical questions – the one that James regarded as the 'most pregnant' question there is – is the one concerning the very existence of the world as such. Why is there something rather than nothing?[47] Jonas also discusses this 'mystery of mysteries' and suggests that there being a world at all is not necessary.[48] Refusing to find consolation in some obscure theory about the alleged necessity of existence goes well together with the moral refusal to find consolation in theodicies. Moreover, it is possible to appreciate the theological, ethical, and existential seriousness of these refusals without making any final metaphysical commitment to the thesis about the contingency of all existence.

Mortality and morality – and the craving for immortality

Just like ethics and metaphysics, also human mortality and morality are, according to Jonas (and, arguably, James), deeply interconnected. Our mortality is, more specifically, a ground of ethics in the sense that there can be no ethics – for us mortals – without a realization of our mortality, just like there can be no life at all without death. This theme was already briefly touched upon above in relation to the significance of the grave as a human artifact in the emergence of humanly distinctive reflection on metaphysics, history, and culture. In another essay, Jonas speaks about the double character of human mortality both as a burden and a blessing.[49] Our mortality is a burden in its 'continual possibility' – we could die at any time – but a blessing in its 'ultimate necessity' – because there would, and could, be no life at all without death.

Indeed, life and death are two sides of the same coin, inseparably tied together. The price of mortality must be paid by the natural process of

DOI: 10.1057/9781137412669.0006

life. This is a metaphysical necessity but it also has an ethical dimension already from the very beginning. When comparing the 'balance sheet' of the total misery and happiness in the world, we should carefully listen to the victims of life, those who have suffered most.[50] James also, as was noted above, exclaimed that we should never be deaf to the 'cries of the wounded.'[51] However, even though the sum of misery may far outweigh the sum of happiness or enjoyment, we should, according to Jonas, avoid drawing the conclusion that it would be better if there were no life at all.[52] This is what he says: 'The presence of *any* worthwhileness in the universe at all [...] immeasurably outweighs *any* cost of suffering it exacts.'[53]

This strikes me as far too strong, however. It is certainly imaginable that *some* 'costs' – some enormous sufferings, or potential sufferings – would be too great to justify the worthwhileness of *any* existence. However, at the meta-level, we can argue for such a view only from within a form of life valuing human existence, and existence as such. The proper pragmatic response to this situation is, it seems to me, a Jamesian meliorism. However bleak the situation of humankind may be, we should always do our best to make it better, while fully understanding that there is no guaranteed happy end – and while also understanding that there are at least imaginable cases in which it might be better for all life to cease to exist. For example, to invoke a Jamesian example derived from Dostoevsky, if the happiness of the entire humankind could be 'bought' at the expense of the eternal torment of a single innocent soul, we would never be morally justified in entering into such a bargain.[54]

Even so, the blessing of mortality, according to Jonas, is that it (and it only) enables what Hannah Arendt called 'natality,' the opening of new perspectives on the world situated within some particular historical contingencies.[55] We have all been born, and through new births there will be new ways of seeing the world, of seeing it for the first time. As Jonas puts it, 'just as mortality finds its compensation in natality, conversely natality gets its scope from mortality.'[56] Mortality is 'the very condition of [...] separate selfhood.'[57] Without natality, we would not be the contingent individuals we are – 'new' in relation to whatever existed before us – and without mortality there would be no natality. Similarly, James's celebration of 'novelty,' 'chance,' and an open, pluralistic universe are contextualized within his serious concern with our finitude, fragility, and utter contingency.[58]

Still, we would hardly be humans if we did not have any need to transcend our mortal, finite condition. According to Jonas, our immortality lies 'in the deed.' This is, arguably, ultimate pragmatism: our moral choices and actions eventually determine the significance of our lives from the perspective of eternity. This doctrine of the immortality of deeds rather than souls amounts to something more than the Tolstoyan and/or Wittgensteinian idea of 'living in the present moment.'[59] It is living in the present moment understood precisely as a commitment to the *moral demandingness of that moment* that makes (if anything makes) us immortal.

'In *moments of decision*,' Jonas tells us, 'when our whole being is involved, we feel as if acting under the eyes of eternity.'[60] This is also where mortality and immortality, the end of time and eternity, meet: our acting 'under the eyes of eternity' is also acting as if the moment of the act were the last one. Our freedom emerges from this 'existential now':

> Swiftly reclaimed by the movement it actuates, it marks man's openness to transcendence in the very act of committing him to the transience of situation, and in this double exposure, which compounds the nature of total concern, the 'moment' places the responsible agent between time and eternity.[61]

There is a certain Kantian ring to this. As is well known, Kant rejected metaphysical theories of the survival of an immortal soul but saved the concept of immortality as a 'postulate of practical reason.'[62] However, even while the ethical point of view is already primary in Kant's discussion of immortality, given Kant's rejection of rationalistic metaphysical theories of the soul, he was still concerned with the immortality of the person (or the soul, ethically interpreted). In contrast, Jonas, by sharpening the primacy of the ethical, deals only with the immortality of our deeds, with the possibility that our 'deeds inscribe *themselves* in an eternal memoir of time.'[63] The total commitment of deed, but also experiences such as the 'call of conscience' or the 'agony of remorse,' may be 'the only empirical signs of an immortal side to our being which our present critical consciousness will still be ready to consider in evidence.'[64]

Our deeds are, then, 'immortalized' in the sense that 'when our whole being is involved in what we are doing we may feel that we are acting "under the eyes of eternity"'.[65] However, this immortality of human deeds is 'for God's sake, not our own'; it is our way of caring about the divine and about the gift of life we have received.[66] In an important way, this very seriousness of morality and the possibility of the meaningfulness of life depend on our fundamental finitude – that is, on mortality rather

DOI: 10.1057/9781137412669.0006

than immortality.[67] In the 'awesome impact of his deeds on God's destiny [...] lies the immortality of man.'[68]

Analogously, James's speculations on immortality[69] arguably depend on his more fundamental concern for the finitude of human life. The very significance of the pragmatic method in philosophy may be ultimately based on our taking seriously the finitude – that is, mortality – of our natural human existence.[70] Only insofar as the potential future experiences in terms of which we should, according to the pragmatic method, examine the meanings of our concepts and ideas are finite (that is, only if there is no infinite number of them to be expected) can we so much as attach any specific meaning to our concepts. Even so, however important our mortality is for the very possibility of human thought and action as we know it, the crave for immortality – in some symbolic sense at least – is so natural to us that we need to address the possible immortality of those whose deeds could never be immortalized.[71] Again, Jonas's concern is profoundly ethically motivated:

> What about those who never could inscribe themselves in the Book of Life with deeds either good or evil, great or small, because their lives were cut off before they had their chance, or their humanity was destroyed in degradations most cruel and most thorough such as no humanity can survive? I am thinking of the gassed children of Auschwitz,[72] of the defaced, dehumanized phantoms of the camps, and of all the other, numberless victims of the other man-made holocausts of our time. Among men, their sufferings will soon be forgotten, and their names even sooner. Another chance is not given them [...]. [Yet] this I like to believe: that there was weeping in the heights at the waste and despoilment of humanity; that a groan answered the rising shout of ignoble suffering, and wrath – the terrible wrong done to the reality and possibility of each life thus wantonly victimized, each one a thwarted attempt of God. 'The voice of thy brother's blood cries unto me from the ground': Should we not believe that the immense chorus of such cries that has risen up in our lifetime now hangs over our world as a dark and accusing cloud?[73]

We must – and this is an ethical 'must' – avoid conceptualizing the 'immortality of deeds' in such a manner that only the active agents have a claim to immortality. If this concept has any significance today, it should be available to those victims of (painfully immortalized) evil deeds whose blood cries up to the 'heights,' those whose 'long-gone cry to a silent God'[74] we have a duty to listen to, including those potential witnesses of historical horrors who did not live to witness and whose testimony we therefore cannot hear.[75] There is certainly a tension in

DOI: 10.1057/9781137412669.0006

Jonas at this point. Perhaps it could be resolved by applying the Jamesian 'democratic' account of immortality, but at this point this remains mere speculation.

A possible disagreement: ethics and metaphysics again

I have identified a number of important points of contact, somewhat overlapping fundamental agreements, between James (or pragmatism more generally) and Jonas. However, I want to conclude this chapter by drawing attention to one very significant disagreement, which is closely connected with a theme already discussed, the relation between ethics and metaphysics. According to Jonas, ethics must be ontologically grounded – recall, for instance, what was said about metabolism above. However, according to James, ontology or metaphysics itself must, ultimately, be ethically grounded. This, indeed, is what it means to apply the pragmatic method to ontological issues. So there is a conflict, or at least a tension, here.

This is not at all to say that a Jamesian-Jonasian pragmatist should not engage in metaphysics. Thus, I do not share exactly the worry raised by Lawrence Vogel in his introduction to Jonas's *Mortality and Morality*. What Vogel points out is that a pluralistic culture may not be able to 'bear the burden' of the kind of 'substantive metaphysics' that Jonas invites us to embrace: 'If our future depends on citizens agreeing with Jonas's speculations, then I fear we are not up to the task.'[76] Bernstein's position is, I think, preferable: Jonas – as well as, in my view, James – may have been able to show that, *pace* Levinas, there is a way of developing naturalistic ontology (or metaphysics) that does not reduce alterity to 'the same' and is able to successfully counter nihilism.[77]

A promising synthesis of the two approaches would perhaps be the view that neither ontology nor ethics is the fundamental ground of the other. They are, rather, both ineliminable from our full philosophical anthropology. They ground and are grounded by each other, reciprocally containing each other. They may even ultimately be one and the same pursuit. Ethics *is* metaphysics, and vice versa, with no 'grounding' either way. The very notion of grounding employed by Jonas may be problematic. If there is any grounding at work here at all, both may be grounded in our need to take evil seriously.

DOI: 10.1057/9781137412669.0006

Insofar as both Jonas and James could be (re-)read in this manner, their possible disagreement might be resolved within their much deeper and ethically much more important anti-theodicist agreement.[78] Be that as it may, despite the (actual or possible) differences between Jonas and James regarding the specifics of the relation between ethics and metaphysics, both can, it seems to me, very well agree about the ultimate purpose of philosophical inquiry; it is, indeed, right here that ethics and metaphysics are deeply intertwined. Writing on Heidegger's unforgivable collaboration with the Nazis, Jonas, his pupil, argues that this biographical fact is inelinably related to Heidegger's philosophy, not just something external to his philosophical work:

> Since ancient times philosophy, unlike every other branch of learning, has been guided by the idea that its pursuit shapes not only the knowledge but also the conduct of its disciples, specifically in the service of the Good, which is after all the goal of knowledge. [...] Therefore, when the most profound thinker of my time fell into step with the thundering march of Hitler's brown battalions, it was not merely a bitter personal disappointment for me but in my eyes a debacle for philosophy. Philosophy itself, not only a man, had declared bankruptcy.[79]

James, perhaps fortunately, did not live to witness this bankruptcy. Yet, had he philosophized in the same historical context in which Jonas was led to his thoughts on theology as a luxury of reason, he might have ended up with many similar ideas. The two philosophers' fundamental agreement – even in the context of the final disagreement I have located – about philosophy being in the service of the good is traceable back to its Kantian sources: it is in the end the practical use of reason that guides reason in *all* its uses, including the theoretical use. If the philosopher does not learn, or does not even care to learn, how to live, s/he is a failed philosopher, irrespective of how profound her/his theoretical reflections on metaphysics, epistemology, ethics, or religion may be. A philosophy as deep as Heidegger's can be ruined because of its author's attachment to one of the most inhuman ideologies of human history.

Conversely, a philosophy that may not reach the theoretical depths of Heidegger – such as, possibly, James's or Jonas's – could, and perhaps should, be held in the highest esteem precisely because of its sincere contribution to the on-going struggle for humanity in the context of contingency, fragility, and metaphysical insecurity. And similarly, a philosophy whose arguments move through negations, focusing (as we have done) on topics

DOI: 10.1057/9781137412669.0006

like evil and suffering, may and should also in the end be in the service of the good, by guiding us in our attempts to live better.

Notes

1 William J. Gavin, '*Pragmatism* and Death: Method vs. Metaphor, Tragedy vs. the Will to Believe', in Stuhr (ed.), *100 Years of Pragmatism*, pp. 81–95.

2 Cf. William James, 'Human Immortality' (1898), in James, *Essays on Religion and Morality*.

3 More generally, pragmatism, as I see it, is a philosophy that should continuously enter into creative and constructive, albeit critical, dialogues with other philosophical perspectives and approaches. See Pihlström (ed.), *The Continuum Companion to Pragmatism*.

4 See Craig, *Levinas and James*.

5 For his explorations of James and pragmatism, see Richard Bernstein, *The Pragmatic Turn* (Cambridge: Polity Press, 2012); for a discussion of Jonas and evil, see Bernstein, *Radical Evil*, chapter 7. Bernstein rarely explicitly connects pragmatism with his views on evil; see, however, Bernstein, *The Abuse of Evil*, for a defense of a pragmatically (also partly Jamesian) approach to evil avoiding dogmatic commitments to any neat bifurcation between the good and the evil. Note, furthermore, that I do not invest any special significance in the notion of 'Continental philosophy'; the pragmatist should of course oppose the received dichotomy between analytic and Continental thought.

6 Hans Jonas, *Mortality and Morality: A Search for the Good after Auschwitz*, ed. Lawrence Vogel (Evanston, IL: Northwestern University Press, 1996).

7 See the essay, 'Evolution and Freedom: On the Continuity among Life-Forms', in Jonas, *Mortality and Morality*, pp. 59–74.

8 Lawrence Vogel, 'Editor's Introduction: Hans Jonas's Exodus: From German Existentialism to Post-Holocaust Theology', in Jonas, *Mortality and Morality*, pp. 1–40 (here p. 15). Jonas more comprehensively deals with natural existence and the responsibility it yields in some of his previous books (not to be discussed here), including especially Hans Jonas, *The Phenomenon of Life: Toward a Philosophical Biology* (New York: Delta, 1966) and Jonas, *The Imperative of Responsibility: In Search of an Ethics for the Technological Age* (Chicago: University of Chicago Press, 1984). (The posthumous volume, *Mortality and Morality*, also contains a bibliography of Jonas's writings.)

9 Vogel, 'Introduction', p. 36. See also Jonas's essay, 'Toward an Ontological Grounding of an Ethics for the Future', in Jonas, *Mortality and Morality*, pp. 99–112.

10 Vogel, 'Introduction', p. 18.

DOI: 10.1057/9781137412669.0006

11   Dewey, *A Common Faith*. Bernstein notes (*Radical Evil*, p. 189) that 'Jonas's
      naturalism bears a strong affinity with the evolutionary naturalism of Peirce
      and Dewey', but he does not mention James in this context.
12   On pragmatism and environmental ethics, see Eric Katz and Andrew Light
      (eds), *Environmental Pragmatism* (London and New York: Routledge, 1996).
13   See Hans Jonas, 'Tool, Image, and Grave: On What Is beyond the Animal in
      Man,' in Jonas, *Mortality and Morality*, pp. 75–86.
14   For a pragmatist analysis of the human capacity to construct and use tools,
      and its philosophical significance, see, for example, John Dewey, *Experience
      and Nature* (1929) (Chicago and La Salle, IL: Open Court, 1986). Heidegger's
      Sein und Zeit (1927) famously contains the discussion of the *Zuhandensein*
      ('being-ready-to-hand') of the world to the Dasein. See Martin Heidegger,
      Sein und Zeit (Tübingen: Max Niemeyer, 1961).
15   Jonas, *Mortality and Morality*, p. 79.
16   Ibid., p. 84.
17   Jonas, *Mortality and Morality*, p. 85. James, as far as I know, nowhere
      deals with graves in any detail, but it does seem to me that this Jonasian
      formulation is well compatible with his view on metaphysics as a study of
      ultimate questions emerging from our puzzlement regarding there being
      anything at all. (Cf. below.)
18   The concept of transaction is preferable to the concept of interaction
      because the latter still invokes two separate poles that interact (that is,
      the organism and the environment, or the subject and the object). To get
      rid of this closet Cartesianism troubling much of modern naturalism, the
      Deweyan naturalistic pragmatist views transaction as a process involving the
      organism in its environment without making any fundamental metaphysical
      separation between the two. Jonas's ethics of life could be seen as adopting
      the Deweyan line here.
19   Douglas Davies, personal communication. Davies's recent views are available
      in, for example, Douglas Davies and Hannah Rumble, *Natural Burial*
      (Basingstoke: Palgrave Macmillan, 2012).
20   Hans Jonas, 'The Burden and Blessing of Mortality,' in Jonas, *Mortality and
      Morality*, p. 89. See also p. 135. On Jonas's concept of metabolism, see also
      Bernstein, *Radical Evil*, p. 190.
21   On the reality of relations, the classical Jamesian reference is William James,
      Essays in Radical Empiricism (1912), in *The Works of William James* (1977). For
      an insightful reading of James's views on relationality, see Medina, 'James on
      Truth and Solidarity'.
22   See Bernstein, *Radical Evil*, especially p. 194ff. As Bernstein puts it (speaking
      about Jonas and Levinas): 'Both categorically reject any philosophical or
      religious attempt to "reconcile" us to evil. They would agree that we must
      give up both vulgar and sophisticated forms of "the Happy End". There

DOI: 10.1057/9781137412669.0006

is something brute, unsurpassable, and "transcendent" about evil, which challenges and defies philosophical concepts and categories.' (Bernstein, *Radical Evil*, p. 203; see also p. 229.) I see no reason why this would not also aptly describe James's position. See also the anti-theodicy discussion in Chapter 1.

23   See again James, *Pragmatism*, pp. 20–2, as well as Chapter 2.

24   Hans Jonas, 'Immortality and the Modern Temper', in Jonas, *Mortality and Morality*, pp. 118–19.

25   See also the brief comments on James's 'realistic spirit' in Chapters 1 and 2. Compare Agamben's comment on 'the aporia of Auschwitz' as the facing of '[f]acts so real that, by comparison, nothing is truer; a reality that necessarily exceeds its factual elements' (*Remnants of Auschwitz*, p. 12).

26   James, *Pragmatism*, chapter 7. (This theme is already present in James's psychological *magnum opus*, *The Principles of Psychology* [1890], also available in *The Works of William James* [1982].) See also the discussion of realism and pragmatic pluralism in Chapter 2.

27   By this phrase we do not have to mean what Levinas means when he regards our ethical duty toward the other as something that is 'otherwise than being', irreducible to ontology. See Emmanuel Levinas, *Otherwise than Being or Beyond Essence* (1969), trans. Alphonso Lingis (Pittsburgh: Duquesne University Press, 1974). As Bernstein demonstrates, this is one of the major differences between Levinas's and Jonas's views on evil: Jonas, unlike Levinas, does not claim that we must give up ontology (metaphysics) in order to arrive at an ethical response to evil (see Bernstein, *Radical Evil*, especially pp. 191, 202). James, on my reading, shares Jonas's rather than Levinas's view here.

28   Hans Jonas, 'Is Faith Still Possible?', in Jonas, *Mortality and Morality*, p. 159.

29   Hans Jonas, 'The Concept of God after Auschwitz', in Jonas, *Mortality and Morality*, p. 133.

30   On James's debates with Bradley in particular, see T.L.S. Sprigge, *James and Bradley: American Truth and British Reality* (Chicago and La Salle, IL: Open Court, 1993).

31   William James, 'Is Life Worth Living?', in James, *The Will to Believe*, p. 55.

32   Vogel, 'Introduction', p. 22.

33   Ibid., pp. 26, 33.

34   Ibid., p. 35.

35   Jonas, *Mortality and Morality*, pp. 134–5, 142.

36   Ibid., pp. 136–8. Jonas adds that in Job's suffering God himself suffers (Jonas, *Mortality and Morality*, p. 143).

37   Jonas, *Mortality and Morality*, p. 138.

38   Ibid., pp. 139–40. For a helpful comparison of Jonas's rethinking to some other Jewish proposals to 'limit' divine omnipotence, see Berel Lang,

'Evil, Suffering, and the Holocaust,' in Lang, *Post-Holocaust: Interpretation, Misinterpretation, and the Claims of History* (Bloomington: Indiana University Press, 2005), pp. 32–51. Bernstein also offers an illuminating discussion of Jonas's non-omnipotent, suffering, and becoming God that is to some extent dependent on us (*Radical Evil*, pp. 196–9).

39 See the essay, 'Is Faith Still Possible?'.

40 Both James's approach to evil and Jonas's rethinking of God after the Holocaust could also be fruitfully compared to Richard Kearney's anatheism, in which the same idea of a self-limiting God, or better, a 'post-God' of 'radical powerlessness,' is invoked again. 'The God that died in Auschwitz was the God of theodicy,' Kearney tells us, and continues: 'Post-Holocaust faith does not believe that God could have stopped the torture – and didn't.' See Kearney, *Anatheism*, especially chapter 3 (the quotes are on pp. 58, 61). What Kearney calls anatheism is neither theistic nor atheistic but a kind of open space leaving the possibility of faith open after the disappearance of the traditional theistic God – largely as a result of the irresolvable problem of evil.

41 See Vogel, 'Introduction,' p. 16.

42 James defends this melioristic middle path between optimism and pessimism in chapter 8 of *Pragmatism*. On Jonas's philosophy as a response to 'modern nihilism,' see Bernstein, *Radical Evil*, pp. 187–8.

43 However, it has been argued by Peter Dews – insightfully invoking Jonas – that it is more difficult to get rid of the theological vocabulary associated with the problem of evil than some secularized thinkers suppose. See Dews, 'Disenchantment and the Persistence of Evil: Habermas, Jonas, Badiou,' in Alan D. Schrift (ed.), *Modernity and the Problem of Evil* (Bloomington: Indiana University Press, 2005), pp. 51–65.

44 Vogel, 'Introduction,' p. 36.

45 See the famous essay, 'The Will to Believe' (1896), in James, *The Will to Believe*, chapter 1.

46 Ludwig Wittgenstein, *Culture and Value*, trans. Peter Winch (Oxford: Basil Blackwell, 1980), pp. 46, 46e (a remark written c. 1944).

47 For James's discussion of this question and its pregnancy, see James, *Some Problems of Philosophy*, chapter 1.

48 Jonas, *Mortality and Morality*, pp. 128–9.

49 Hans Jonas, 'The Burden and Blessing of Mortality,' in Jonas, *Mortality and Morality*, pp. 87–98.

50 Jonas, *Mortality and Morality*, p. 93.

51 James, 'The Moral Philosopher and Moral Life,' in *The Will to Believe*. See also Ruth Anna Putnam's discussion of this Jamesian idea, for example, in her 'The Moral Life of a Pragmatist,' in Owen Flanagan and Amelie Oksenberg Rorty (eds), *Identity, Character and Morality* (New York: Brandford Book, 1990), pp. 67–89.

DOI: 10.1057/9781137412669.0006

52   We should, in my view, react with horror to attempts to argue in all
     philosophical seriousness for such a conclusion, as, for example, in David
     Benatar, *Better Never to Have Been: The Harm of Coming into Existence* (Oxford:
     Oxford University Press, 2006). For a criticism of Benatar's nihilistic ethics of
     extinction, see Pihlström, *Transcendental Guilt*, chapter 4.

53   Jonas, *Mortality and Morality*, p. 94 (my emphasis).

54   See again James's influential paper, 'The Moral Philosopher and the Moral
     Life.' One of the most sustained discussions of the importance of this essay I
     am familiar with is Franzese, *The Ethics of Energy*.

55   Jonas, *Mortality and Morality*, p. 95. For the concept of natality, see Hannah
     Arendt, *The Human Condition* (Chicago: University of Chicago Press, 1958).

56   Jonas, *Mortality and Morality*, p. 96.

57   Hans Jonas, 'Immortality and the Modern Temper,' in Jonas, *Mortality and
     Morality*, p. 126.

58   Moreover, both Jonas and the pragmatists would be opposed to emergent
     novelty in the sense of a mysterious leap: there is also continuity in the world,
     and any adequate theory of natality should acknowledge this. See Bernstein,
     Radical Evil, p. 263 (n13). In pragmatism, continuity is a more Peircean than
     Jamesian theme; indeed, it is the key notion of Peirce's 'synechism.' See again
     Pihlström, *Pragmatist Metaphysics*, chapter 6.

59   See Wittgenstein, *Tractatus*, § 6.4311.

60   Jonas, *Mortality and Morality*, p. 120.

61   Ibid., p. 121.

62   This basic Kantian argument is formulated in Kant's *Critique of Practical
     Reason* (*Kritik der praktischen Vernunft*, 1788), available in, for example, Kant,
     Werke in zehn Bänden, ed. Weischedel. For an examination of its relation to
     Jamesian philosophy of religion, see Pihlström, *Pragmatic Pluralism and the
     Problem of God*, chapter 1.

63   See Jonas, *Mortality and Morality*, p. 122.

64   Ibid., p. 125.

65   Vogel, 'Introduction,' p. 22.

66   Ibid., p. 23.

67   See Ibid., p. 24.

68   Jonas, *Mortality and Morality*, p. 136.

69   See James, 'Human Immortality'.

70   For a development of this theme, see Pihlström, '*The Trail of the Human
     Serpent Is over Everything*', chapter 3.

71   Compare this to James's defense of a 'democratic' conception of
     immortality – contrasted to an 'aristocratic' one – in 'Human Immortality'.

72   Note Jonas's repeated references to *children* – both in the dark context of
     Auschwitz and in the more positive (albeit related) one of developing an
     ethics of responsibility in which the nurturing of responsibility itself is

DOI: 10.1057/9781137412669.0006

transmitted from a generation to another. The concepts of children and childhood in Jonas's philosophy, connected with the Arendtian notion of natality, would deserve a separate extended discussion.

73 Jonas, *Mortality and Morality*, p. 129.

74 Ibid., p. 131.

75 On this deeply troubling feature of testimony, and the related impossibility of (full, complete) testimony, see Agamben, *Remnants of Auschwitz*. See also Agamben's reflections on the meaninglessness and anonymity of deaths in the camps, for example, pp. 70–2, 104.

76 Vogel, 'Introduction,' p. 6.

77 Bernstein, *Radical Evil*, especially p. 202.

78 We should note, however, that it is not generally agreed that Jonas actually succeeds in his anti-theodicism. Giorgio Agamben, another perceptive philosopher discussing the camps, claims that Jonas is one of those who confuse law and morality, as well as law and theology, in the end proposing 'a new theodicy.' The 'conciliatory vice of every theodicy,' he argues, is 'particularly clear' in Jonas's account of the powerless God, and according to him Jonas even succumbs to the temptations of a 'happy ending' when he suggests that we should now take care that the horrors of Auschwitz will not be repeated. 'Behind the powerlessness of God peeps the powerlessness of men, who continue to cry "May that never happen again!" when it is clear that "that" is, by now, everywhere' (Agamben, *Remnants of Auschwitz*, p. 20). This is a deeply troubling critique, and I am not quite convinced that it makes justice to Jonas's sincere attempt to move beyond theodicies. Even so, we should continue to be aware of the constant challenge of avoiding pseudo-theodicist happy endings in our 'never again' cries, and learn to perceive the ubiquitous reality, or at least the traces, of 'that' that we want to prevent from ever happening again.

79 Jonas, 'Philosophy at the End of the Century,' in *Mortality and Morality*, p. 49.

DOI: 10.1057/9781137412669.0006

4
A Metaphilosophical Conclusion

Abstract: *This final chapter returns to the concept of recognition, already invoked in Chapter 1 in relation to the issue of theodicy. The anti-theodicist argumentation of the entire book can be summarized by maintaining that the victims of evil are not recognized as victims in an ethically adequate manner if the evil they suffer is rendered allegedly meaningful in terms of a theodicy. The distinction between recognition and acknowledgment is then emphasized. Finally, the pragmatist ethics developed in the book is metaphilosophically characterized by employing the basic idea of holistic pragmatism, as developed by Morton White. The chapter concludes with a treatment of the relation between the philosophizing individual and her/his philosophical view. Any pragmatically adequate account of evil must address the individual 'philosophical temperament' seeking to understand evil.*

Keywords: recognition; acknowledgment; relativism; holistic pragmatism; James, W.; White, M.; Feyerabend, P.

Pihlström, Sami. *Taking Evil Seriously*. Basingstoke: Palgrave Macmillan, 2014. DOI: 10.1057/9781137412669.0007.

DOI: 10.1057/9781137412669.0007

We should now draw some main threads of the overall argument of this book together. Hilary Putnam suggested three decades ago in 'Why Reason Can't Be Naturalized'[1] that there are two key forms of *naturalized epistemology* available in recent philosophy: first, reductive naturalism or physicalism, derived from the natural sciences, and secondly, cultural relativism, derived from anthropology. The problem with both, he argues, is that they give up *genuine normativity*. Something similar happens with naturalized ethics: sacrificing genuine normativity of philosophical inquiry into the good life by reducing the object of that inquiry into mere moral behavior, as explained in terms of, for example, cognitive processes or cultural codes of behavior, is the price we have to pay for being scientifically plausible in the sciences of morality. Even though I have not at all attempted to argue against any well-established scientific facts in this book, it seems to me that if my reflections in the previous chapters are even close to being on the right track, such 'naturalizing' projects are not philosophically serious engagements in ethics. (This does not mean, of course, that ethics would be anything non-natural.) What ethics truly needs, instead of both cultural relativism and scientistic attempts at naturalization, is a 'negative' awareness of the seriousness of evil, suffering, humiliation, and violations of dignity.

I have, at least implicitly, argued against different forms of reductionism in philosophy and in favor of *pluralism* as well as pragmatic, anti-foundationalist cooperation between fields like anthropology and philosophy in our continuing conversation on topics like good and evil. What I see myself as having been doing in this book is, therefore, a kind of philosophical anthropology. (At least that is the closest I can get to classifying my work in terms of philosophical sub-disciplines.) However, if we want to truly develop philosophical anthropology, or the philosophy of the human condition, today, we must get rid of sharp, essentialist divisions of labor. This is one of the reasons for which I have proposed that we should turn to pragmatism, especially James, in order to appreciate our key task in philosophy, especially philosophical anthropology, as the task of *learning to listen to all the relevant voices*, or at least to as many voices as possible, including voices from empirical anthropology, the history of philosophy, systematic philosophical analysis, and most importantly the real victims of empirical historical evils. If our philosophizing about evil is not relevant to human beings in agony, then it is not relevant at all. As Wittgenstein wrote,[2] when a human being feels her-/ himself to be lost, that is *die höchste Not*.

DOI: 10.1057/9781137412669.0007

On the other hand, all the way from the beginning I have admitted that a certain degree of relativism can, and should, be accepted in comparative (for example, anthropological) studies of the good. There is no universal or absolutely correct conception of human flourishing; Jamesian (and Deweyan) pragmatists should be among the first to insist that ideals of the good are tied to local environments, cultural contexts, and other such backgrounds that give shape to our lives. But I have also argued that the reality of evil is harsher and more dramatic, and that there can be no genuine relativity there. In our encounters with evil, we need to develop a 'realistic spirit.' Relativity is not to be conflated with the real generality that I suggested (in Chapter 1) characterizes evil; nor should generality be conflated with universality, because evil can be general without being universally the same in different contexts.

As distinguished from any allegedly universally good forms of life, the universality of human (and, by extension, non-human) pain and suffering offers a way of overcoming cultural relativism and the related incommensurability of frameworks, schemes, language-games, traditions, and other contextual 'measures' of good and evil.[3] What this universality of pain and suffering gives rise to is a transcontextual ethical normativity and criticism. We may, as I have admitted, hold relativist conceptions of the good, as anthropology (among other human and social sciences) may teach us, but we cannot – either ethically or ontologically – afford to be relativists or anti-realists about suffering, or, hence, about evil. This is also one reason why ethics and ontology are fundamentally linked. To be sure, evil is part of the 'natural history of human forms of life' (to employ a Wittgensteinian expression), and as such it does possess a considerable degree of historical variability, but this by no means restricts its universal significance. As Hans Jonas points out (as we saw in Chapter 3), the wasted human bodies and distorted faces of the camps may be among the *most real* things there are in the world we live in; what we philosophically owe to the victims, and to all sufferers, is a realistic account of evil. This requires, I have suggested, a 'negative' philosophical method. We have to start from the *shock* of the reality of evil and develop our more positive ethics on that basis, realizing that ethics can no longer be based on any positive value or principle[4] – which immediately leads to the further observation that there is, in the end, no 'basis,' 'ground,' or 'foundation' at all for ethics other than the ethical perspective itself, understood as a continuous reaction to the shock of evil.

DOI: 10.1057/9781137412669.0007

Yet, this focus on the brute reality of evil and suffering does not imply that evil would not itself be historically conditioned. On the contrary, precisely in its historical multifariousness – it takes ever new forms – evil is so shocking. It is brute and shocking in its reappearance and non-articulability in novel (including entirely banal) situations and historical circumstances. It is, as Arendt observed, the banality of evil itself that is 'unsayable and unimaginable.'[5]

Recognition and acknowledgment

It is also because of the ever changing historical circumstances in which evil may be or become real that we need to cultivate our abilities to *recognize* human suffering and victims of evil in their status as sufferers. Instead of seeking to offer any theological or philosophical 'solutions' to the problem of evil, my purpose in this book has been to clarify the discussion around this problem (or set of problems) by showing how the pragmatic method can be sharpened into a method of 'negative think-ing.' Now, this methodological reflection may be carried one step further by explicitly employing the concept of recognition (already briefly intro-duced in Chapter 1). More precisely, the concept of recognition should be used in a distinctively *pragmatic* sense, even though explicit discus-sions of recognition have been rare in the pragmatist tradition.[6] What we may mean by 'pragmatic recognition' is the recognition of someone – a person or a group – in some practical role, that is, as (an) actor(s) or agent(s) of a certain kind or as (a) subject(s) involved in certain norma-tively structured practices or habits of action.[7]

Of course, recognition, in the Hegelian tradition of *Anerkennung*, re-established in more recent philosophy by Axel Honneth and many others, is always a matter of recognizing someone *as* something. What the notion of pragmatic recognition contributes to this general picture is the specific recognition of someone as an agent of certain kind, that is, as a subject involved in certain practices or habits of action (understood in a pragmatist sense). The 'as' clause, that is, is specified in terms of the actions, habits, and/or practices the recognized person or collective engages in. These may be formal or official, as in the case of recognizing, say, a person in some particular public role with the rights and duties that office entails. But, more importantly for the topics we have discussed in this book, they can also be highly informal and unofficial. One way of

DOI: 10.1057/9781137412669.0007

summarizing my investigation so far is to say that I have tried to inquire into the necessary (transcendental) conditions for an *ethically adequate recognition* of certain people – individuals or groups – and especially for their recognition as victims of certain instances of evil and suffering, particularly of persecution and atrocities such as, paradigmatically, the Holocaust.[8] This way of understanding what I am now calling pragmatic recognition requires a broadening of the notion of 'agent' relevant to the specification of the 'as' clause: a passive victim or sufferer is also an agent in the relevant sense, going through an experiential process with a certain specific meaning or significance (or, often, an experience characterized by a complete lack of meaning).[9] Conversely, we have also critically discussed (already in Chapter 1) the ways in which victims of evil and suffering could recognize, or fail to recognize, philosophically 'well-meaning' theodicies. The challenges of adequate recognition cut into several directions.

I find the concept of recognition potentially helpful in this area because the philosophical discourse surrounding the problem of evil is extremely polarized. Not only do the rival views sharply disagree with each other; in many cases they either fail to talk to each other or may even disregard each other completely. I am not saying that the concept of recognition, or any other philosophical concept, would easily resolve this situation. On the contrary, as has become clear, I also have my own favorite ('anti-theodicist') views in this field, and I cannot claim to have been able to fully recognize all relevant rival perspectives. However, I do think that the concept of recognition may serve the common interest of identifying the most plausible positions and facilitating a philosophical dialogue between them.

One of our core questions here is whether, say, a Holocaust survivor (or victim) or, more theoretically, an anti-theodicist thinker could ever *recognize* (even well-meaning) attempts to justify the reality of evil, or to 'accommodate' evil into a harmonious world-picture. Conversely, the question is whether we can say that a theodicist following, say, Marilyn McCord Adams's argument (see Chapter 1 above) actually *recognizes* the person or people who, as sufferers or as victims of evil, have had to go through the unspeakable kind of suffering that the Holocaust involved. The question of recognition runs through this entire discussion and therefore still needs to be addressed in some detail.

I would be prepared to argue that the Holocaust victim does not get proper recognition as a victim in any theodicist theory, including

DOI: 10.1057/9781137412669.0007

Adams's. S/he might be recognized as someone who seeks, and possibly finds, meaning in her/his life after the horror participation, but still s/he fails to get recognition as a victim or sufferer. The only ethically adequate recognition would be the 'handing back of the ticket,' to repeat Ivan Karamazov's famous words.[10] Because *such* recognition is lacking in Adams, her contribution (in turn) may not and perhaps cannot be fully recognized by the anti-theodicist as a serious, or even as an ethically decent, contribution to the discussion.

The problem may lie in Adams's strongly metaphysical notion of 'perfect goodness' (or divine goodness), according to which 'the divine essence is maximally, indeed infinitely and immeasurably, excellent.'[11] It is in terms of such divine perfection that horror participation, according to Adams, is finally compensated for, even if never rendered meaningful in itself. Invoking such a metaphysically perfect divine essence in this way is not only to beg the question against those who find the existence of evil incompatible with any such essence but is also an insult to those who try to keep on believing in God after Auschwitz, possibly in a rethought way (following, for example, Jonas and James, for whom God needs to be rethought as finite instead of infinite and omnipotent, as shown in Chapter 3). A proper recognition of the victims of atrocities *qua victims* requires, then, an ethical ground upon which any metaphysical goodness is based. *This* is missing from Adams's theory. I would suggest, and have at least implicitly suggested in the previous chapters, that a version of such an ethical ground can be found in pragmatism, especially in James's pragmatism, in which ethical and metaphysical perspectives are inseparably entangled, as we have seen.

However, the notion of (mutual) pragmatic recognition may be helpful not only in locating the true bone of the controversy but also in seeking ways out. When genuinely attempting to recognize each other not only as actual or potential victims or sufferers but also, more theoretically, as participants of the same community of ethical reflection and inquiry, we may to some extent tolerate our theoretical differences over the possibility and desirability of a theodicy and focus on engaging, and perhaps healing, the victims. Let me therefore very briefly introduce the perspective that the concept of recognition may offer us here, especially in relation to pragmatist approaches to the problem of evil in the philosophy of religion.

It is important to note that issues of recognition are not restricted to the mutual recognition among persons or groups (for example, representing

DOI: 10.1057/9781137412669.0007

different religious or non-religious outlooks) as being epistemically or rationally entitled to their (religious or non-religious) views, but extend to the need to recognize, from the perspective of certain intellectual and/ or ethical outlooks, certain ethically significant *limitations* or *boundaries* that define the proper sphere of human experience, cognition, or reason-use, and even to the need to recognize different groups and people as actual or potential 'recognizers' of quite different boundaries. The diverging ways in which, say, theists and atheists or theodicists and anti-theodicists recognize something as a boundary limiting human capacities should themselves be recognized by both groups – in a way that not merely tolerates these different boundaries but acknowledges that there may be legitimately different ways of drawing them, without simply agreeing with the other party, either.

Various acts of recognition across the boundary dividing, for example, religious believers and non-believers may have as their content at least the following different types of recognition: one party may recognize the other as (i) human beings (for example, with certain inviolable human rights), as (ii) thinkers capable of formulating thoughts and/or judgments with intelligible content, as (iii) actual or potential participants in political discussion and deliberation, and/or as (iv) 'fellow inquirers' (for example, possibly, philosophers) seeking the truth about the matter at issue (for example, about God's existence or non-existence, or about the nature and meaning of evil). These different specifications and qualifications of the content of the act of recognition involve quite different factual and normative commitments and expectations. For example, recognizing someone as a fellow inquirer in the pursuit of truth yields expectations significantly stronger than 'merely' recognizing the same person or group as member(s) of the human species, or even as sharing a common humanity in some stronger sense invoking, say, fundamental human rights. The different contents of acts of recognition may be crucially related to the concept of rationality: we may recognize someone as rational (for example, as an inquirer) while disagreeing with her/him on fundamental issues – but can we also consistently disagree about the criteria of rationality itself?

A key meta-level issue in contemporary philosophy of religion is the very possibility of critical discussion of religious beliefs, including religious beliefs about evil and suffering (and their actual or potential meaningfulness or meaninglessness). In order for such discussion to be possible across the boundary dividing believers and non-believers,

DOI: 10.1057/9781137412669.0007

both groups must in some sense recognize each other as members of the same intellectual and ethical community – as rational discussion partners – and thus in a sense overcome or at least reconsider the boundaries dividing them from each other. Now the same obviously applies to theodicist and anti-theodicist believers (and non-believers).[12] The pragmatist philosopher's job in this situation is to examine critically the conceptual, practice-laden presuppositions for the possibility of the relevant kind of recognition acts. For a pragmatist, such presuppositions are always inevitably practice-embedded – in short, habits of action.

To continue the analogy drawn from the philosophy of religion: if, for example, Christian believers and 'new atheists' are able to recognize each other ethically, politically, and/or intellectually, can they also recognize each others' entitlement to a membership in the same community of inquirers (a community that is, arguably, itself normatively constituted by mutual acts of recognition)? That is, can they recognize each other *as* 'fellow inquirers' committed to the pursuit of truth? Could they do this even while maintaining very different normative conceptions of the role of reason, objectivity, and evidence in the evaluation of religious thought and beliefs, recognizing quite different (both factual and normative) limits for human thought and capacities? Examining these questions pragmatically, employing the notion of recognition, can be expected to lead to rearticulations of several traditional issues in the philosophy of religion, including the problem of evil.

Now, if a relation of mutual recognition is in some sense possible for Christians and new atheists, is it also possible for theodicists and anti-theodicists? It seems to me that the ethically relevant divide between these two positions may cut even deeper and may therefore make ethically genuine recognition across this boundary very difficult. The reason for this is that from the anti-theodicist point of view, the theodicist justification of evil is a fundamental violation to the sufferers' moral right to reject any pseudo-justification or pseudo-explanation of why they had to suffer.

Recognizing philosophical and/or theological positions and their advocates as intellectual systems of thought and as rational persons must be distinguished from another kind of recognition, the recognition of persons (and peoples) as sufferers, or as victims of various types of evil and atrocities, such as violence, murder, or genocide. Both are instances of pragmatic recognition, as they are related to certain human actions, habits of action, and capacities for action, but the types of action they

DOI: 10.1057/9781137412669.0007

presuppose are quite different, that is, intellectual theorization on the one hand and more practical responses to suffering on the other hand. The notion of pragmatic recognition draws attention to this variability of the practice-involving contexts that play a crucial role in shaping the 'as' in the notion of recognizing someone as something. An intellectually highly sophisticated exchange of theoretical ideas on evil may be based on mutual recognition among the disagreeing participants, while still failing to adequately recognize the victims those theoretical ideas refer to, or their suffering. Thus, an argumentative exchange on evil might be theoretically highly fruitful yet entirely lacking in pragmatic recognition.

In brief, while a free will theodicist following Plantinga or Swinburne, or a van Inwagenian 'defense' theorist, or an Adamsian 'beatific compensation' theodicist (see Chapter 1), may be recognized by an anti-theodicist at an intellectual level where the relevant practices are intellectual and theoretical (and vice versa), the relevant kind of recognition may be lacking at the more practical level where a Holocaust survivor (implicitly) asks for recognition as a victim who has gone through unspeakable suffering. Here the 'as' is different, and appreciating this pragmatic difference is crucial for a proper understanding of the problem of evil.

We have seen that, when the challenge of recognizing victims of evil as victims (or, more neutrally, as sufferers) is taken seriously, theodicies arguably turn out to be crude forms of non-recognition. This is a way of summarizing the entire argument of this book, even though my Jamesian formulations have employed a rather different language. We should also re-emphasize that the concept of (pragmatic, mutual) recognition employed here crucially invokes the 'as' clause: someone or some group is always recognized as something. Recognition is not a relation between equals – and this is one reason why the entire issue is not only ethically but also politically problematic. The party granting recognition to the party requesting recognition is in some sense in an authoritative position. A well-meaning 'recognition' of someone as a victim of, say, the Holocaust might itself also – in a certain specific context – amount to a non-recognition of that person in some other social role, specified by some other 'as' clause. In some cases and for some purposes, it might actually be better to speak about the recognition of certain forms of suffering, instead of continuing to operate in terms of the recognition of certain people (persons) as victims. This permanent possibility

DOI: 10.1057/9781137412669.0007

of mis- or non-recognition is itself a major element of our attempt to continue reflecting on evil.[13]

For these reasons, the argument could be taken one step further by asking whether the 'as' clause itself could or should be dropped in some cases of fundamental human importance. Here an important distinction could be drawn between the concepts of recognition and *acknowledgment*.[14] The way I would like to draw this distinction emphasizes the asymmetry between recognition and acknowledgment regarding the 'as' clause in particular: there is no specific 'as' in acknowledgment, except perhaps in the very basic sense of the acknowledged person or group being entitled to something like our common humanity, and thus there is no need to ask for, search, or request recognition as anything specific, either. Moreover, in acknowledgment there is no need for the kind of hierarchical order there almost inevitably is between the parties requesting and granting recognition. The party granting acknowledgment is in no authoritative position in relation to the party acknowledged, and it is, slightly paradoxically, through this acknowledgment itself that the non-authoritative status is indicated.

Furthermore, while recognition is based on someone's seeking recognition as something and thus on at least some kind of common conceptual ground between the subject and object of recognition, acknowledgment involves no such necessity of conceptual (let alone ethically or politically hierarchical) pre-categorization of the acknowledged person or group as something, or anything, in particular (viz., as something else than merely 'other'). Recognition is a matter of recognizing someone as something in particular, with these two poles of the relation in a sense inhabiting the same conceptual world, but this need not be the case with acknowledgment. While recognition may be needed especially in situations in which we have (to put it in a Wittgensteinian manner) reached the bedrock[15] and are unable to rationally argue with the other anymore (that is, when we have lost hope of reaching agreement but are still committed to something more than the mere toleration of the other's diverging views), the question inevitably arises whether we can always recognize the other when s/he is *very* far from us.[16] Do we first have to understand in order to be able to recognize? Here it could be suggested that we can acknowledge the other, without the 'as' clause, even when we have no way of really understanding what her/his perspective on the world is, and how, hence, the 'as' clause could be specified.

DOI: 10.1057/9781137412669.0007

Furthermore, while recognition is fundamental for normative social theory, because acts and relations of (mutual) recognition largely normatively constitute social institutions and social reality in the sense we are familiar with them,[17] acknowledgment is a fundamental ethical experience or perspective opening toward the other *as other*. Such an other, possibly a victim of past evil and suffering very far from us, is a limit to our subjectivity itself, demonstrating our own finitude and the resulting infinite task of ethical acknowledgment.[18] Thus, in sum, while recognition deals with *finite* and well-structured social reality, acknowledgment deals with the *infinity* of one's, or my, ethical duty toward the other. One might argue that it is, in the end, the latter that makes the problem of evil the fundamental problem it is for us. At least the reflections on evil in this book have been offered from the perspective of the 'infinitely demanding' task of ethical reflection.[19]

It could even be suggested that the theodicist tendency to fail to recognize suffering in its brute reality and equally brute meaninglessness and pointlessness – the failure to develop a 'realistic spirit' in this area of philosophical reflection – is itself an example of what Arendt called the banality of evil.[20] Non-acknowledgment too easily penetrates into our most well-meant and religiously or ethically sophisticated attempts to face evil. Facing evil, even facing it philosophically, is not just a matter of philosophical argumentation, understood as mere business as usual. Instead, it is something that ought to shake our lives in a fundamental way. This is why we need an ethical critique of the philosophy of religion focusing on evil, that is, a critique of discourses on evil that fail to acknowledge the suffering other or tend to swipe her/his suffering under the carpet of cool rational theorization. The banality of evil may in this sense be found right in the middle of the theodicy discussion itself.

Perhaps silence, instead of theoretical reflection, is, then, the only acceptable form of acknowledgment. But the nagging question returns: is it, really? Or should we, rather, continue to speak about evil, inevitably fallibly and incompletely, without any final resolutions or theoretical justifications? And in what kind of language should we seek to do this? These questions do not seem to terminate at any specific point, but we do seem to have the obligation to at least philosophically investigate the conditions for the possibility of still writing philosophy, poetry, and theology after Auschwitz – which is something I have attempted to do in this book.

DOI: 10.1057/9781137412669.0007

Holistic pragmatist metaphilosophy

It still needs to be clarified what kind of an attempt this has been. Therefore, I want to, by way of concluding, add some reflections of a more metaphilosophical kind that might illuminate the nature of the philosophical investigation needed, and to some extent engaged in here. I hope these final reflections will also help to specify in what sense my approach in this book has been a *pragmatist* one – to the extent that my proposed method of negative thinking is itself an elaboration of the pragmatist method. In other words, I want to (re-)acknowledge the metaphilosophical character of my reflections throughout the book. This entire undertaking has largely been a critical discussion of *what kind of philosophy is morally appropriate in the world we live in*. Therefore, it has in a sense been a pragmatist attempt to philosophize ethically about philosophy itself, including ethics and philosophy of religion in particular. Now, what *is* metaphilosophy, and how can it be conducted? And what difference does this make for the kind of inquiry pursued in this book?

Metaphilosophy could – at least in principle – be defined as the 'philosophy of philosophy,' along the lines of 'philosophy of X,' where the variable 'X' can stand for virtually any human practice, discourse, or field of activity (such as 'science,' 'art,' 'culture,' 'religion,' or 'sport'). As there is no definite limit to what kinds of practice or discourse can be philosophically analyzed and examined, why shouldn't 'X' also be able to take the value 'philosophy'? However, is metaphilosophy an independent area of philosophical inquiry? Could someone, say, specialize in metaphilosophy in the way in which one may legitimately specialize in the philosophy of science (or, as is increasingly common, in one of its more narrowly defined sub-fields, such as the philosophy of physics, the philosophy of economics, the philosophy of biology, and so on), the philosophy of art, or the philosophy of religion?

It has sometimes been argued that metaphilosophy can enjoy no independent existence in the way other fields of philosophical inquiry can and do. On the other hand, it is highly questionable to suppose that *any* philosophical field of inquiry could be independent of the others. Here we should go beyond the obvious mutual dependencies of, say, logic and the philosophy of language, or moral and political philosophy. Even apparently distinct sub-fields of philosophy such as metaphysics and ethics are profoundly dependent on each other (as has also been

DOI: 10.1057/9781137412669.0007

proposed in this book), because ethical theories may have metaphysical presuppositions (for example, concerning the nature of personhood) while metaphysical theorizing itself may be ultimately based on our ethical orientation in the world, as pragmatists like James plausibly maintain.[21] Similarly, for instance, the philosophy of religion and epistemology are mutually dependent: systematic work in the philosophy of religion to a large extent amounts to epistemological exploration of the rational justification of theistic (or atheistic) claims. Philosophy generally, then, may be seen as the 'coordinating' field of inquiry within which all these more special, mutually dependent inquiries fall. As a 'field,' it is *dynamic*, rather than static: one's commitments in one sub-field may crucially affect the possible commitments one may make in another sub-field.

Now, I do not believe that metaphilosophy could be the foundational or 'grounding' sub-discipline of philosophy any more than philosophy itself can act as the foundation or ground of all other fields of inquiry. From a non-reductively naturalistic perspective, philosophy and the various empirical disciplines are parts of the same overarching 'web of belief' (to use a well-known expression we owe to W.V. Quine, without being committed to any specific Quinean view about philosophy or anything else). Philosophy and the sciences are in the same business of explaining and understanding the world, as has been argued by holists and naturalists at least since Quine's famous 'Two Dogmas.'[22] Any alleged 'first philosophy' according to which philosophy is an autonomous discipline over and above to, or more fundamental than, the sciences, ought to be rejected – while also rejecting the reductive view, which radical Quinean naturalists are often tempted to maintain, that philosophical issues are nothing but scientific or empirical issues. The metaphor of a dynamic field, or the Quinean notion of a holistic web of belief, is useful here quite independently of the specific difficulties that Quine's own brand of naturalism may face.

Now, it may be suggested that the relation between metaphilosophy (as a part of philosophy) and philosophy generally is analogous to the relation between philosophy (as a part of human inquiry) and inquiry generally. Metaphilosophy is the inevitably dynamically changing and continuously transformed and self-transforming element of the dynamic field of philosophical inquiry that reflects on the nature of philosophical inquiry itself, its purpose, methods, possible objects, and so forth, just like philosophy generally may reflect on the purpose, methods, possible objects, and so on, of inquiry more generally (including both scientific

DOI: 10.1057/9781137412669.0007

and everyday inquiry). It is that kind of inquiry that the present book has been concerned with.

Instead of Quinean reductive naturalism (or eliminativism), the *holistic pragmatism* developed by Morton White, one of the most important but unfortunately neglected pragmatist philosophers of the twentieth (and twenty-first) century, offers us a useful tool for explicating the relation between metaphilosophical and 'first-order' philosophical statements and reflections. Just as factual and ethical (or descriptive and normative) statements are, according to White, parts of the same holistic 'web', critically tested as a holistic totality with no sharp dichotomy between the descriptive and the normative,[23] it may be suggested that metaphilosophical and 'first-order' philosophical statements constitute a holistic web that must also be evaluated as a totality, not by evaluating its individual components on a case-by-case basis. It is impossible to isolate a purely metaphilosophical element in the web, one that would involve no 'first-order', substantial philosophical component; conversely, it is equally impossible to isolate a mere first-order, non-metaphilosophical piece of philosophical thought that would involve no implicit conception of what philosophy itself is. Note also that this need not mean that it is, in order to engage in metaphilosophical reflection (such as the reflection of this book), necessary to be committed to certain specific first-order philosophical theses or views; the notion of 'component' need not here be conceived in this way. Rather, what is necessary is an awareness of problems, as well as of potentially relevant considerations for their possible solution. For example, a genuine awareness of the depth of the problem of evil – rather than any specific view on how it should be solved – is, in my view, needed for the kind of metaphilosophical reflection on negative thinking and ethics that I have engaged in here.

That is, one's metaphilosophical commitments are – and cannot help being – profoundly entangled with one's commitments in 'first-order' areas of philosophical inquiry and reflection. For example, when one espouses a certain view in epistemology, one should also consider the nature of philosophical inquiry and philosophical knowledge in terms of that general epistemological position. When one believes something metaphysical about the nature of persons, or human beings, one must consider the implications of those beliefs on one's conception of philosophizing as an activity those beings engage in. Metaphilosophy is thus always already built into philosophy itself. Whenever one engages in philosophical concept-formation, theorizing, reflection, and

DOI: 10.1057/9781137412669.0007

inquiry – systematically or historically – one also inevitably engages in metaphilosophizing. And conversely, when metaphilosophizing, one always already philosophizes. In principle, an indefinite hierarchy of meta-meta-meta-...-philosophies could be constructed, but that would hardly make any sense, given that 'mere' metaphilosophy already presupposes philosophy itself and may, when reflecting on philosophy, also reflect on its own status and role within philosophy.

Clearly, then, we should firmly reject the view that there can be such a practice as 'mere' metaphilosophizing, that is, philosophical inquiry into philosophy itself that is not, and does not presuppose, any philosophical views on anything else but philosophy itself. Such metaphilosophy would be *empty*, but 'mere' philosophizing without a reflective metaphilosophical 'level' would be *blind*. This Kantian metaphor is as illuminative here as it is in Kant's own epistemological view concerning the entanglement of concepts and intuitions. This book has not attempted to draw any metaphilosophical moral about the ethical status of certain philosophical approaches in the absence of substantial discussions of evil, nor, however, have I attempted to say anything about evil at a metaphilosophically neutral level.

This general picture of metaphilosophical inquiry, spelled out in terms of White's holistic pragmatism, which can be plausibly developed into a holistic non-reductive pragmatic naturalism and pragmatic philosophical anthropology, is of course itself metaphilosophical. As any metaphilosophical reflection, it presupposes first-order philosophical views and arguments, in this case specifically pragmatist (and non-reductively naturalist) views concerning human concept-formation and belief-fixation. These, again, can and should be investigated both systematically and historically. The history of philosophy is a fundamentally important element of any (meta)philosophical web of belief worth taking seriously – and this, again, is itself a metaphilosophical statement about the nature of philosophy. Conversely, again, the history of philosophy can function as an element of our metaphilosophical web of belief only insofar as it is dynamically entangled with work in systematic philosophy. From a pragmatist point of view, it is neither desirable nor even possible to maintain any dichotomy between the history of philosophy and systematic philosophy. Holistic entanglement applies here, too.

Moreover, *this* general picture of metaphilosophy is *not* a neutral umbrella under which any kind of philosophical methodology whatsoever could be accommodated. For instance, the kind of holistic pragmatism used here as a meta-level framework for the (meta-meta-philosophical?) development of the defended kind of (meta-)meta-philosophical picture of the relation between metaphilosophy and (mere) philosophy does preclude a number of philosophical methodologies, including crude eliminative materialism (physicalism), extreme post-modernist relativism, Wittgensteinian-inspired (but arguably not genu-inely Wittgensteinian) merely grammatical conceptions of 'therapeutic' philosophy, and many others – none of which can be discussed here any further, of course. Metaphilosophizing by no means presupposes philosophical neutrality. It is, rather, continuous critical and self-critical reflection on the philosophical inquiry one engages in together with other inquirers. Pragmatism is of course only one possible framework for such inquiry, but suitably developed it is a very promising one. And evil, of course, is only one possible test case for this kind of inquiry, but as I have tried to argue, it is a kind of crucial experiment for the ethical and existential adequacy of philosophy.

'Who touches this book touches a man'

Finally, we should metaphilosophically reflect on the relation between the *philosophizing human being* – the philosophizing individual – and the philosophical and metaphilosophical activities s/he engages in. This demand adds a further dimension to our on-going task of recognition. We should (metaphilosophically) recognize, or better, acknowledge, the human person – the inevitably socially engaging individual – at the center of any philosophical activity, including in particular the philo-sophical inquiry into evil.

As James famously maintained in the opening of *Pragmatism*, the history of philosophy is to a large extent a history of clashes of philosoph-ical temperaments. Metaphilosophically, and holistically, we may find it necessary to pragmatically consider – and perhaps critically judge – not only the philosophical ideas explicitly subscribed to by a philosopher but also, within the same total 'system' of that person's philosophical commit-ments, the kind of life s/he leads in various areas of human engagement. Striking examples could be taken up here: consider, for example, the famous case of Heidegger's Nazism (cf. Chapter 3), or the other some-what less famous thinkers who made the unforgivable mistake of joining the most destructive political movement of the twentieth century.[24]

DOI: 10.1057/9781137412669.0007

How should we evaluate these thinkers' 'total philosophy' (the 'man plus ideas')? As Jonas points out, he felt that with Heidegger's (who was, after all, his teacher) Nazism 'philosophy itself', not just the man, had 'declared bankruptcy' (see the conclusion to Chapter 3). Now, this holistic totality, *person-cum-ideas*, could, I would like to suggest, be evaluated in terms of holistic pragmatism: not just the ideas, not only the person, but the total system is the 'unit' of critical evaluation.

Let me address this issue by briefly returning to the Jamesian issues discussed toward the end of Chapter 2. Even though philosophizing – about topics such as evil, in particular – is a deeply personal project, I have argued that pragmatist inquiry into these issues must *not* lead to radical relativism.[25] A Jamesian pragmatist believer in disunity and disbeliever in ('theodicist') eventual harmony must be able to replace Feyerabendian anarchism captured in the infamous 'anything goes' slogan by more responsible philosophical commitments that preserve the possibility of drawing normative distinctions between good and evil.[26] So, let us conclude by focusing on the following Jamesian ideas.

In his 1891 essay, 'The Moral Philosophy and the Moral Life', James urged: 'Don't be deaf to the cries of the wounded!' – as has already been noted above several times. The cries of the wounded – the (unintended) victims of our pragmatic attempts to experimentally develop our practices and habits of action – are among the (abundant, rich) 'voices' of reality that we must hear, and learn to hear better, instead of reducing them away from the eventual harmony. There is a sense in which these voices set us a demand to action, not letting us rest. The theodicist, on the contrary, *is* deaf to the cries of the wounded, reducing evil and suffering away.[27]

James also famously maintained that '[t]he trail of the human serpent is [...] over everything.'[28] This is his appeal for the ultimately human character of all world-categorizations. There is no final ontological categorization of the world as it is in itself. The world we live in is a human world, and we are *responsible* not only for what we do in the world but also for how we categorize it. We are, therefore, responsible for acknowledging the suffering of the victims as ultimately and irreducibly real.

Consider, finally, the phrase James (mis)quotes from Walt Whitman's poem, 'So Long!', in *Pragmatism*: 'who touches this book touches a man.'[29] This quote, which I want to metaphilosophically emphasize as a key to the very issue concerning the 'holistic totality' of an individual human being and her/his philosophical commitments, occurs in the context of

James's discussion of individual philosophical temperaments that 'with their cravings and refusals do determine men in their philosophies, and always will.'[30] The correct Whitman quote, as the editors of the volume explain, is this: 'Camerado! This is no book; Who touches this, touches a man.'[31] The fundamental idea, once again common to James and Feyerabend, here seems to be that our 'books' – that is, whatever philosophical, scientific, ethical, political, aesthetic, or any other perspectives on the world we produce – are not just neutral descriptions of reality but expressions of our individuality, among the abundant 'voices' that need to be heard by human beings, whether they engage themselves with science, art, politics, religion, or whatever.

That is, we must – as has been argued throughout the book – take seriously both our human finitude, the fact that we are radically limited beings, and the insight that any perspective on the world (including any book produced and/or read by us) is a human achievement, rather than a privileged representation of a perspective-independent reality. This is also to take seriously our fallibility, which is part of our finitude. The world cannot be known by finite beings like us as a totality from a God's-Eye-View but can be experientially approached in its historically unfolding abundance. Such experiences of abundance and of the diversity of our possible human perspectives on the world should be ethically extremely significant for us. Moreover, they are also, partly because of their ethical significance, metaphysically (and possibly even theologically or religiously) significant.

The alleged 'arch-relativist' Feyerabend, especially in his late period, insisted on the 'openness of cultures', contrasting this idea with the relativistic view that cultures or conceptual systems are 'closed' and isolated.[32] In fact, relativism and its key rival, (scientific) realism, share the assumption that 'traditions' are 'well defined and clearly separated.'[33] Instead, Feyerabend urges, cultures and traditions are open to each other – to the world they are embedded in: *potentially every culture is all cultures.*[34] This is, arguably, primarily because evil and suffering challenge us to ethical seriousness regardless of our culturally contextualized ideas of the good. Pragmatist insistence on finitude and fallibilism, on the one side, and Feyerabend's anti-relativistic (yet also non-realist) 'openness' view, on the other, go very well together. Without being open to otherness – to other cultures or traditions as well as to other individuals' philosophical temperaments – and without genuinely seeking to hear what they have to tell us, we cannot fully recognize our own finitude, which is something

DOI: 10.1057/9781137412669.0007

we need to recognize in order to adequately understand the richness of the world around us. It is only through appreciating our own finitude and fallibility that we can learn to appreciate the significance of the abundance of other perspectives on the world. More importantly, our openness to otherness – in the spirit of 'negative thinking' – is primarily openness to others' suffering, actual and potential, as well as to our own failures of ever adequately responding to it.

Developing this idea systematically would, however, require a much more comprehensive discussion. Let me just close with the thought that philosophers', like anyone else's, catastrophic involvement with, for instance, Nazism – or evil more generally – is not just historically but also philosophically and metaphilosophically of utmost importance, a historical voice never to be forgotten. Understanding our own actual or potential involvement in evil, our transcendental guilt, is a crucial part of taking evil seriously.

Notes

1   This essay is available in Hilary Putnam, *Realism and Reason* (Cambridge: Cambridge University Press, 1983).
2   See Wittgenstein, *Culture and Value*, pp. 46, 46e.
3   Incommensurability, of course, is a key notion in the philosophy of science, largely thanks to Feyerabend's seminal contributions (cf. the discussion of Feyerabend in Chapter 2). Here I will not be able to analyze this notion. I am using it only in contrast to the points made about evil; instead of saying that experiences of evil – or suffering in general – would fall on a 'commensurate' or 'commensurable' scale of experiences, we might say that the very issue of incommensurability does not (yet) arise in that context. Evil is more fundamental.
4   Compare Agamben's remark that 'Auschwitz marks the end and the ruin of every ethics of dignity and conformity to a norm' (*Remnants of Auschwitz*, p. 69).
5   Hannah Arendt, *Eichmann in Jerusalem: A Report on the Banality of Evil* (London: Penguin, 1992; first published 1963), p. 252. See also Agamben, *Remnants of Auschwitz*, p. 21.
6   While pragmatism and recognition theories have only seldom been connected, the notion of pragmatic recognition is actually used in Kevin S. Decker, 'Perspectives and Ideologies: A Pragmatic Use for Recognition Theory', *Philosophy and Social Criticism* 38 (2012), 215–26. For an attempt to develop a

broadly pragmatist philosophy of religion in which the concept of recognition plays a key role, see Sami Pihlström, 'Objectivity in Pragmatist Philosophy of Religion,' forthcoming in *Nordic Studies in Pragmatism* (www. nordprag.org).

7   In this book, I am obviously unable to discuss the already massive, and growing, literature on recognition that has followed Axel Honneth's seminal work, *Kampf um Anerkennung* (Frankfurt am Main: Suhrkamp, 2003; first published 1992). A useful overall discussion of recognition is available online in the *Stanford Encyclopedia of Philosophy*: see Mattias Iser, 'Recognition' (2013), http://plato.stanford.edu/entries/recognition/. Regarding the relevance of recognition to the philosophy of religion, I am particularly indebted to Risto Saarinen, 'Anerkennungstheorien und ökumenische Theologie,' in Thomas Bremer (ed.), *Ökumene – überdacht* (Quaestiones disputatae 259, Freiburg: Herder, 2013), pp. 237–61.

8   Note that we may talk about the recognition of certain persons as victims as well as about the recognition of victims as persons, or human beings. (In the literature on the Holocaust, it has often been noted that even the recognition of the victims' basic humanity, their belonging to the human species, may have been denied to them in the camps; see again Agamben, *Remnants of Auschwitz*, chapter 2.) It might also be advisable to avoid the conceptual category of 'victim' altogether in this context, because in many cases victimization may be ethically highly problematic. I have rather loosely spoken (and will continue to speak) about 'victims of evil' or 'victims of suffering' without defining the notion of a victim in any formal way, and without claiming that it would always be ethically unproblematic or politically correct to use such vocabulary. In fact, my concluding discussion on the difference between recognition and acknowledgment (see below) will propose one way of moving beyond the need to recognize victims as something specific.

9   Compare this to what was said about James's and Levinas's similar ideas of activity vs. passivity in Chapter 2.

10 Cf. the brief discussion of Dostoevsky's *The Brothers Karamazov*, partly based on Susan Neiman's arguments (see her *Evil in Modern Thought*), in Chapter 1.

11 Adams, 'Ignorance, Instrumentality, Compensation, and the Problem of Evil', p. 25.

12 In order for such discussions to extend to ethical and political matters related to religion, the rival groups must also recognize each other as belonging to the same moral and political community. However, we should avoid drawing another sharp limit between intellectual matters, on the one side, and moral or political ones, on the other; this division plays only a heuristic role here.

13 In any event, the act of recognition is inevitably a response to a request for recognition, as analyzed (in the theological context) in Saarinen,

DOI: 10.1057/9781137412669.0007

'Anerkennungstheorien und ökumenische Theologie'. In some cases, the request itself may of course be highly implicit, or the need for any such request may itself only arise as a response to an experience (possibly by a third party) of there being a failure in recognition.

14   I adopt the concept of acknowledgment from Stanley Cavell; see his *The Claim of Reason*. The concept has also been interestingly used by Putnam, for example, in his *Philosophy in an Age of Science*, where Putnam – a Cavell-influenced philosopher – speaks about continuous possibilities of non-acknowledgment. The more specific conceptual relations between the discourse on recognition around Honneth et al. and the discourse on acknowledgment around Cavell and other Wittgenstein-inspired thinkers would certainly deserve more scrutiny. We might say – although I am not making historical or interpretive claims here – that Levinas's ethics of otherness is also based on a notion of acknowledgment (rather than recognition). For a brief comparison between Levinas and Cavell in this regard, see Simon Critchley's 'Introduction' to Simon Critchley and Robert Bernasconi (eds), *The Cambridge Companion to Levinas* (Cambridge: Cambridge University Press, 2002), especially pp. 30–2; see also Putnam's contribution, 'Levinas and Judaism', in the same volume. Note, furthermore, that my way of using the notion of acknowledgment (indebted to Cavell and Levinas) differs from the way in which the notion is contrasted to recognition in, for example, Arto Laitinen 'Recognition, Acknowledgement, and Acceptance', in Heikki Ikäheimo and Arto Laitinen (eds), *Recognition and Social Ontology* (Leiden: Brill, 2011), pp. 309–48.

15   See Wittgenstein, *Philosophical Investigations*, Part I, § 217.

16   For a recent insightful Wittgenstein-inspired contribution to this discussion of understanding – and criticizing – the 'other', primarily drawing on Wittgenstein's *On Certainty* (1969), see Cora Diamond, 'Criticising from "Outside"', *Philosophical Investigations* 36 (2013), 114–31. The issues of cultural relativism, diverging standards of rationality, and so on, would again be relevant here but must be left for another occasion.

17   See Honneth's *Kampf um Anerkennung* and Iser's 'Recognition' for more details on this, and see Saarinen's 'Anerkennungstheorien und ökumenische Theologie' for reflections on the relevance of these constitutive relations to religion and ecumenics.

18   Even the 'Muselmann', as analyzed by Holocaust writers like Primo Levi (see again Agamben, *Remnants of Auschwitz*, chapter 2), would – while remaining at the boundary separating the human from the non-human – be a potential object of acknowledgment, though (and this is a special horror of the camps) no longer of recognition.

19   See again Critchley, *Infinitely Demanding*.

20   See Arendt, *Eichmann in Jerusalem*.

DOI: 10.1057/9781137412669.0007

21 Cf., again, Pihlström, *Pragmatist Metaphysics*, for some further reflections on this.

22 See W.V. Quine, 'Two Dogmas of Empiricism' (1951), chapter 2 in Quine, *From a Logical Point of View*, rev. edn (Cambridge, MA and London: Harvard University Press, 1980; 1st edn 1953).

23 See, for example, Morton White, *Toward Reunion in Philosophy* (Cambridge, MA: Harvard University Press, 1956) and *A Philosophy of Culture: The Scope of Holistic Pragmatism* (Princeton, NJ: Princeton University Press, 2002). See also Pihlström (ed.), *The Continuum Companion to Pragmatism*.

24 On the deeply puzzling theme of philosophers' engagement with Nazism, see Yvonne Sherratt, *Hitler's Philosophers* (New Haven, CT and London: Yale University Press, 2012) as well as Hans-Jörg Sandkühler (ed.), *Philosophie im Nationalsozialismus* (Hamburg: Felix Meiner, 2009).

25 As remarked in the introduction and again in the beginning of this chapter, anthropology can in my view end up with relativism about the good (as conceptualized in different cultures or societies); the universal significance of evil and suffering prevent this move in morally serious philosophy. Relativism – at least radical relativism – about evil is ethically unacceptable because it fails to recognize the sheer shock of victims' horror. Furthermore, because full-blown moral relativism would have to include relativism about evil as well as about the good, moral relativism in that sense cannot be accepted.

26 Even though, admittedly, James himself, in the first lecture of *Pragmatism*, describes the pragmatist as an 'anarchist,' 'happy-go-lucky' kind of creature.

27 It might be added that another way of being 'deaf' is to be in the grip of a scientistic ideology according to which individual responsibility can be transferred to an impersonal scientific world-picture. However, 'our science is a drop, our ignorance a sea,' as James memorably put it in *The Will to Believe*. We should always take seriously the *finitude* of our scientific and other intellectual endeavors. The more our scientific knowledge grows, the more there is for us to ask further questions about. Science produces not only knowledge but further questions and problems, further ignorance. It should, therefore, produce humility instead of hubris (as it often does).

28 James, *Pragmatism*, p. 37.

29 Ibid., p. 24.

30 Ibid.

31 Ibid., p. 151.

32 Feyerabend, *The Conquest of Abundance*, p. 78.

33 Ibid., pp. 122–3, 215.

34 Ibid., pp. 215–16; see also p. 240.

DOI: 10.1057/9781137412669.0007

Bibliography

Adams MM. 'Ignorance, Instrumentality, Compensation, and the Problem of Evil'. *Sophia* 52, 2013:7–26.

Adams MM. 'Horrendous Evils and the Goodness of God', *Proceedings of the Aristotelian Society*. 1989, suppl. vol. 63:297–310. Reprinted in Stump E and Murray M, editors, *The Philosophy of Religion: The Big Questions*. Malden, MA and Oxford: Blackwell, 1999. pp. 250–7.

Agamben G. *Remnants of Auschwitz: The Witness and the Archive*, Heller-Roazen D, translator. New York: Zone Books, 2002.

▶ Arendt H. *The Portable Hannah Arendt*. New York: Viking, 2007.

Arendt H. *Eichmann in Jerusalem: A Report on the Banality of Evil*. London: Penguin, 1992 [1963].

Arendt H. *The Human Condition*. Chicago: University of Chicago Press, 1958.

Aristotle. *Nicomachean Ethics*. [Internet] 2013. [cited Dec. 2013]. Available from: www.perseus.tufts.edu.

Armstrong DM. *Truth and Truthmakers*. Cambridge: Cambridge University Press, 2004.

Benatar D. *Better Never to Have Been: The Harm of Coming into Existence*. Oxford: Oxford University Press, 2006.

Bernstein R. *The Pragmatic Turn*. Cambridge: Polity Press, 2012.

Bernstein R. *The Abuse of Evil*. Cambridge: Polity Press, 2005.

Bernstein R. *Radical Evil: A Philosophical Interrogation*. Cambridge: Polity Press, 2002.

Burke FT. *What Pragmatism Was*. Bloomington: Indiana University Press, 2013.

DOI: 10.1057/9781137412669.0008

Camus A. 'Die Krise des Menschen'. *Philosophie Magazin* 11, 2013. [originally in French 'La crise de l'homme'. In: *Camus's Oeuvres completes*, 1965].

Cavell S. *The Senses of Walden*. Chicago and London: University of Chicago Press, 1992 [1971].

Cavell S. *The Claim of Reason*. Oxford: Oxford University Press, 1979.

Colapietro V. 'The Tragic Roots of Jamesian Pragmatism'. *Journal of Speculative Philosophy*, forthcoming.

Cole P. *The Myth of Evil*. Edinburgh: Edinburgh University Press, 2006.

Craig M. *Levinas and James*. Bloomington: Indianapolis, 2011.

Critchley S. *Infinitely Demanding: Ethics of Commitment, Politics of Resistance*. London: Verso, 2007 [paperback edn 2012].

Critchley S. *How to Stop Living and Start Worrying*. Cambridge: Polity, 2010.

Critchley S and Bernasconi R, editors. *The Cambridge Companion to Levinas*. Cambridge: Cambridge University Press, 2002.

Davidson D. *Essays on Actions and Events*. Oxford: Clarendon Press, 1980.

Davies D, Rumble H. *Natural Burial*. Basingstoke: Palgrave Macmillan, 2012.

Decker KS. 'Perspectives and Ideologies: A Pragmatic Use for Recognition Theory'. *Philosophy and Social Criticism*. 2012, 38:215–26.

Dewey J. *A Common Faith*. New Haven, CT and London: Yale University Press, 1991 [1934].

Dewey J. *Logic: The Theory of Inquiry*. In: Boydston JA, editor. *The Collected Works of John Dewey: The Later Works*. Vol. 12. Carbondale: Southern Illinois University Press, 1986 [1938].

Dewey J. *Experience and Nature*. Chicago and La Salle, IL: Open Court, 1986 [1929].

Dewey J. *The Quest for Certainty: A Study on the Relation between Knowledge and Action*. Boston: G.P. Putnam's Sons, 1960 [1929].

Dewey J. *The Problems of Men*. New York: Philosophical Library, 1946.

Dews P. *The Idea of Evil*. Malden, MA: Blackwell, 2008.

Dews P. 'Disenchantment and the Persistence of Evil: Habermas, Jonas, Badiou'. In: Schrift AD, editor. *Modernity and the Problem of Evil*. Bloomington: Indiana University Press, 2005.

Diamond C. 'Criticising from "Outside"'. *Philosophical Investigations*. 2013, 36:114–31.

Diamond C. *The Realistic Spirit*. Cambridge, MA and London: The MIT Press, 1991.

DOI: 10.1057/9781137412669.0008

Feyerabend P. *The Tyranny of Science*. Oberheim E, editor. Cambridge: Polity Press, 2011 [first published in Italian in 1996].

Feyerabend P. *Conquest of Abundance: A Tale of Abstraction versus the Richness of Being*. Terpstra B, editor. Chicago and London: The University of Chicago Press, 1999.

Feyerabend P. *Against Method: An Outline of an Anarchistic Theory of Method*. London: Verso, 1993 [1975].

Franzese S. *The Ethics of Energy: William James's Moral Philosophy in Focus*. Frankfurt: Ontos, 2008.

Gaita R. *Good and Evil: An Absolute Conception*. Rev. edn. London and New York: Routledge, 2004 [1991].

Gaita R. *A Common Humanity*. London and New York: Routledge, 2000.

Gavin WJ. 'Pragmatism and Death: Method vs. Metaphor, Tragedy vs. the Will to Believe'. In: Stuhr J, editor. *100 Years of Pragmatism: William James's Revolutionary Philosophy*. Bloomington: Indiana University Press, 2010. pp. 81–95.

Hämäläinen N. 'Sami Pihlström, Transcendental Guilt: Reflections on Ethical Finitude'. *Journal of Value Inquiry*. 2011, 45(3):373–8.

Heidegger M. *Sein und Zeit*. Tübingen: Max Niemeyer, 1961 [1st edn 1927].

Hobbs CA. 'Why Classical American Pragmatism is Helpful for Thinking about Death', *Transactions of the Charles S. Peirce Society*. 2011, 47:182–95.

Honneth A. *Kampf um Anerkennung*. Frankfurt am Main: Suhrkamp, 2003 [1992].

Hook S. *Pragmatism and the Tragic Sense of Life*. New York: Basic Books, 1974.

Iser M. 'Recognition'. In: *Stanford Encyclopedia of Philosophy*. [Internet] 2013. [cited Dec. 2013] Available from: http://plato.stanford.edu/entries/recognition/.

James W. *The Varieties of Religious Experience: A Study in Human Nature*. Burkhardt FH, Bowers F, and Skrupskelis IK, editors. Cambridge, MA and London: Harvard University Press, 1985 [1902].

James W. *Talks to Teachers on Psychology and to Students on Some of Life's Ideals*. Burkhardt FH, Bowers F, and Skrupskelis IK, editors. Cambridge, MA and London: Harvard University Press, 1983 [1899].

DOI: 10.1057/9781137412669.0008

James W. *Some Problems of Philosophy: A Beginning of an Introduction to Philosophy*. Burkhardt FH, Bowers F, and Skrupskelis IK, editors. Cambridge, MA and London: Harvard University Press, 1979 [1911].

James W. *The Will to Believe and Other Essays in Popular Philosophy*. Burkhardt FH, Bowers F, and Skrupskelis IK, editors. Cambridge, MA and London: Harvard University Press, 1979 [1897].

James W. *Essays in Radical Empiricism*. Burkhardt FH, Bowers F, and Skrupskelis IK, editors. Cambridge, MA and London: Harvard University Press, 1977 [1912].

James W. *A Pluralistic Universe*. Burkhardt FH, Bowers F, and Skrupskelis IK, editors. Cambridge, MA and London: Harvard University Press, 1977 [1909].

James W. *Pragmatism: A New Name for Some Old Ways of Thinking*. Burkhardt FH, Bowers F, and Skrupskelis IK, editors. Cambridge, MA and London: Harvard University Press, 1975 [1907].

Johnston M. *Surviving Death*. Princeton, NJ: Princeton University Press, 2010.

Jonas H. *Mortality and Morality: A Search for the Good after Auschwitz*. Vogel L, editor. Evanston, IL: Northwestern University Press, 1996.

Jonas H. *The Imperative of Responsibility: In Search of an Ethics for the Technological Age*. Chicago: University of Chicago Press, 1984.

Jonas H. *The Phenomenon of Life: Toward a Philosophical Biology*. New York: Delta, 1966.

Kant I. *Kritik der praktischen Vernunft*. In: Weischedel W, editor. *Kant, Werke in zehn Bänden*. Darmstadt: Wissenschaftliche Buchgesellschaft, 1983 [1788].

Katz E, Light A, editors. *Environmental Pragmatism*. London and New York: Routledge, 1996.

Kearney R. *Anatheism: Returning to God after God*. New York: Columbia University Press, 2010.

Kilpinen E. *The Enormous Fly-Wheel of Society: Pragmatism's Habitual Conception of Rationality and Social Theory*. Helsinki: University of Helsinki, Department of Sociology, 2000.

Laitinen A. 'Recognition, Acknowledgement, and Acceptance'. In: Ikäheimo H and Laitinen A, editors. *Recognition and Social Ontology*. Leiden: Brill, 2011. pp. 309–48.

Lang B. 'Evil, Suffering, and the Holocaust'. In: Lang B. *Post-Holocaust: Interpretation, Misinterpretation, and the Claims of History*. Bloomington: Indiana University Press, 2005. pp. 32–51.

DOI: 10.1057/9781137412669.0008

Levinas E. *Otherwise than Being or Beyond Essence.* Lingis A, translator. Pittsburgh: Duquesne University Press, 1974 [1969].

Malpas J and Solomon RC, editors. *Death and Philosophy.* London and New York: Routledge, 1998.

Marchetti S. *The Moral Philosopher: Ethics and Philosophical Critique in William James,* forthcoming.

Margalit A. *The Ethics of Memory.* Cambridge, MA and London: Harvard University Press, 2002.

Medina J. 'James on Truth and Solidarity: The Epistemology of Diversity and the Politics of Specificity'. In: Stuhr JJ, editor. *100 Years of Pragmatism.* Bloomington, IN: Indiana University Press, 2010, pp. 124–43.

Meister C. *Evil: A Guide for the Perplexed.* London: Bloomsbury, 2012.

Misak C. *The American Pragmatists.* Oxford and New York: Oxford University Press, 2013.

Mulhall S. *Faith and Reason.* London: Duckworth, 1994.

Nagel T. *Mortal Questions.* Cambridge: Cambridge University Press, 1979.

Neiman S. *Evil in Modern Thought: An Alternative History of Philosophy.* Princeton, NJ: Princeton University Press, 2002 [paperback edition 2004].

Nelkin DK. 'Moral Luck', In: *Stanford Encyclopedia of Philosophy.* [Internet] 2008 [cited Dec. 2013]. Available from: http://plato. stanford.edu/entries/moral-luck/.

Niiniluoto I. *Critical Scientific Realism.* Oxford and New York: Oxford University Press, 1999.

Niiniluoto I. *Is Science Progressive?* Dordrecht: Reidel, 1984.

Nussbaum M. *Love's Knowledge.* Oxford: Oxford University Press, 1990.

Nussbaum M. *The Fragility of Goodness.* Cambridge, MA and London: Harvard University Press, 1986.

Oberheim E. Feyerabend, Paul K. (1924–1994). In: Shook JR, editor. *Dictionary of Modern American Philosophers.* Bristol: Thoemmes Press, 2005.

Peirce CS. *The Essential Peirce.* 2 vols. The Peirce Edition Project. Bloomington and Indianapolis: Indiana University Press, 1992–98.

Peirce CS. *The Writings of Charles Sanders Peirce.* 7 vols (to date). The Peirce Edition Project, Bloomington and Indianapolis: Indiana University Press, 1980.

DOI: 10.1057/9781137412669.0008

Peirce CS. *The Collected Papers of Charles Sanders Peirce.* Hartshorne C, Weiss P (vols 1–6), and Burks AW (vols 7–8). Cambridge, MA: Harvard University Press, 1931–58.

Phillips DZ. 'The Problem of Evil'. In: Brown SC, editor. *Reason and Religion.* Ithaca, NY and London: Cornell University Press, 1977.

Pihlström S. 'Objectivity in Pragmatist Philosophy of Religion'. *Nordic Studies in Pragmatism*, forthcoming. Available from: www.nordprag. org.

Pihlström S. *Pragmatic Pluralism and the Problem of God.* New York: Fordham University Press, 2013a.

Pihlström S. 'Realism and Pluralism in Pragmatist Philosophy of Religion'. In: Rydenfelt H, Pihlström S, editors. *William James on Religion.* Basingstoke: Palgrave Macmillan, 2013b.

Pihlström S. 'A New Look at Wittgenstein and Pragmatism'. *European Journal of Pragmatism and American Philosophy.* 2012, 4(2). Available from: www.journalofpragmatism.eu.

Pihlström S. *Transcendental Guilt: Reflections on Ethical Finitude.* Lanham, MD: Lexington Books / Rowman & Littlefield Publishing Group, 2011.

Pihlström S, editor. *The Continuum Companion to Pragmatism.* London and New York: Continuum, 2011.

Pihlström S. *Pragmatist Metaphysics: An Essay on the Ethical Grounds of Ontology.* London and New York: Continuum, 2009.

Pihlström S. 'The Trail of the Human Serpent Is over Everything': Jamesian Perspectives on Mind, World, and Religion.* Lanham, MD: University Press of America. Rowman & Littlefield Publishing Group, 2008a.

Pihlström S. 'How (Not) to Write the History of Pragmatist Philosophy of Science?' *Perspectives on Science.* 2008b, 16:26–69.

Pihlström S. 'Religion vs. Pseudo-Religion: An Elusive Boundary'. *International Journal for Philosophy of Religion.* 2007, 62:3–31.

Pihlström S. *Pragmatic Moral Realism: A Transcendental Defense.* Amsterdam: Rodopi, 2005a.

Pihlström S. 'Satujen moraaliopetukset: Mietteitä moraalikasvatuksesta, ansiosta ja armosta' ['The Moral Lessons of Fairy Tales: Thoughts on Moral Education, Merit, and Mercy'], *Kasvatus* 2005b, 36:89–100.

Pihlström S. *Naturalizing the Transcendental: A Pragmatic View.* Amherst, NY: Prometheus/Humanity Books, 2003a.

Pihlström S. 'On the Possibility of Philosophical Anthropology'. *Journal of Philosophical Research.* 2003b, 28:259–85.

DOI: 10.1057/9781137412669.0008

Pihlström S. 'William James on Death, Mortality, and Immortality'. *Transactions of the Charles S. Peirce Society*. 2002, 38.

Pihlström S. 'Death – Mine or the Other's? On the Possibility of Philosophical Thanatology'. *Mortality*. 2001, 6:265–86.

Pihlström S. *Pragmatism and Philosophical Anthropology: Understanding Our Human Life in a Human World*. New York: Peter Lang, 1998.

Pihlström S, Sutinen A. 'William James's Educational Will to Believe'. In: Siljander P, Kivelä A, and Sutinen A, editors. *Theories of Bildung and Growth: Connections and Controversies between Continental Educational Thinking and American Pragmatism*. Rotterdam: Sense Publishers, 2012.

Press E. *Beautiful Souls: The Courage and Conscience of Ordinary People in Extraordinary Times*. New York: Picador, 2012.

Preston J. Paul Feyerabend. In: *Stanford Encyclopedia of Philosophy* [Internet]. 2009 [Dec. 2013]. Available from: http://plato.stanford. edu/entries/feyerabend/.

Putnam H. *Philosophy in an Age of Science*. de Caro M and Macarthur D, editors. Cambridge, MA and London: Harvard University Press, 2012.

Putnam H. *Realism and Reason*. Cambridge: Cambridge University Press, 1983.

Putnam H. *Reason, Truth and History*. Cambridge: Cambridge University Press, 1981.

Putnam RA. 'The Moral Life of a Pragmatist'. In: Flanagan O and Oksenberg Rorty A, editors. *Identity, Character and Morality*. New York: Brandford Book, 1990. pp. 67–89.

Quine V. 'Two Dogmas of Empiricism'. In: Quine V. *From a Logical Point of View*, rev edn. Cambridge, MA and London: Harvard University Press, 1980[1953], pp. 20–46.

Rowe W, editor. *God and the Problem of Evil*. Malden, MA and Oxford: Blackwell, 2001.

Royce J. *The Basic Writings of Josiah Royce*, ed. John J. McDermott (New York: Fordham University Press, 2005).

Saarinen R. 'Anerkennungstheorien und ökumenische Theologie', in Bremer T, editor. *Ökumene – überdacht*. Quaestiones disputatae 259. Freiburg: Herder, 2013. pp. 237–61.

Sandkühler HJ, editor. *Philosophie im Nationalsozialismus*. Hamburg: Felix Meiner, 2009.

DOI: 10.1057/9781137412669.0008

Schrift AD, editor. *Modernity and the Problem of Evil.* Bloomington and Indianapolis: Indiana University Press, 2005.

Sherratt Y. *Hitler's Philosophers.* New Haven, CT and London: Yale University Press, 2012.

Sprigge TLS. *James and Bradley: American Truth and British Reality.* Chicago and La Salle, IL: Open Court, 1993.

Stokhof M. *World and Life as One: Ethics and Ontology in Wittgenstein's Early Philosophy.* Stanford, CA: Stanford University Press, 2002.

Swinburne R. 'The Problem of Evil'. In: Brown SC, editor. *Reason and Religion.* Ithaca, NY and London: Cornell University Press, 1977.

Tilghman B. *An Introduction to the Philosophy of Religion.* Oxford and Cambridge, MA: Blackwell, 1994.

Tillich P. *The Courage to Be,* 2nd edn. New Haven, CT and London: Yale University Press, 2000 [1952].

Todorov T. *The Totalitarian Experience.* Lavender Fagan T, translator. London: Seagull Books, 2011.

Todorov T. *Facing the Extreme: Moral Life in Concentration Camps.* New York: Metropolitan/Holt, 1996.

Tooley M. 'The Problem of Evil'. In: *Stanford Encyclopedia of Philosophy.* [Internet]. 2012 [Dec. 2013] Available from: http://plato.stanford.edu/entries/evil/.

Unamuno M de. *Tragic Sense of Life.* Crawford Flitch JE, translator. New York: Dover, 1954 [originally in Spanish, 1913].

Van Inwagen P. *The Problem of Evil.* Oxford: Clarendon Press, 2006.

Viale C. 'William James' Conception of Religion in Josiah Royce's Mature Thought: Three Approaches', forthcoming.

Viale C. 'Royce and Bernstein on Evil'. *Contemporary Pragmatism* 2013, 10:73–90.

Vogel L. 'Editor's Introduction: Hans Jonas's Exodus: From German Existentialism to Post-Holocaust Theology'. In: Vogel L, editor. *Jonas H. Mortality and Morality.* Evanston, Illinois: Northwestern University Press, 1996. pp. 1–40.

Welzer H. *Täter: Wie aus ganz normalen Menschen Massenmörder werden.* 3rd edn. Frankfurt am Main: Fischer, 2009 [2005].

White M. *A Philosophy of Culture: The Scope of Holistic Pragmatism.* Princeton, NJ: Princeton University Press, 2002.

White M. *Toward Reunion in Philosophy.* Cambridge, MA: Harvard University Press, 1956.

DOI: 10.1057/9781137412669.0008

Willaschek M. 'Bedingtes Vertrauen: Auf dem Weg zu einer pragmatistischen Transformation der Metaphysik'. In: Hartmann M, Liptow J, and Willaschek M, editors. *Die Gegenwart des Pragmatismus*. Berlin: Suhrkamp, 2013. pp. 97–120.

Williams B. *Moral Luck*. Cambridge: Cambridge University Press, 1981.

Winch P. *Trying to Make Sense*. Oxford and New York: Blackwell, 1987.

Winch P. *Ethics and Action*. London: Routledge and Kegan Paul, 1972.

Wisdo D. *The Life of Irony and the Ethics of Belief*. Albany: SUNY Press, 1993.

Wittgenstein L. *Culture and Value*. Wright GH von, editor; Winch P, translator. Oxford: Basil Blackwell, 1980.

Wittgenstein L. *Tractatus Logico-Philosophicus*. Pears DF and McGuinness BG, translators. London: Routledge and Kegan Paul, 1974 [1921].

Wittgenstein L. *Notebooks 1914–1916*. Anscombe E and Wright GH von, editors. Oxford: Basil Blackwell, 1961.

Wittgenstein L. *Philosophical Investigations*. 2nd edn. Anscombe GEM, translator. Oxford: Basil Blackwell, 1958 [1953].

Wright GH von. *Explanation and Understanding*. Ithaca, NY: Cornell University Press, 1971.

Zimbardo P. *The Lucifer Effect: How Good People Turn Evil*. London: Rider, 2007.

DOI: 10.1057/9781137412669.0008

Index

DOI: 10.1057/9781137412669.0009

DOI: 10.1057/9781137412669.0009

DOI: 10.1057/9781137412669.0009

DOI: 10.1057/9781137412669.0009

6.01.15   **DATE DUE**

PRINTED IN U.S.A.